FIX-IT and FORGET-IT®
BAKING
with your
SLOW COOKER

Fix-It and Forget-It®
BAKING
with your
SLOW COOKER

150 Slow Cooker Recipes for Breads,
Pizza, Cakes, Tarts, Crisps, Bars, Pies,
Cupcakes, and More!

New York Times bestselling author
Phyllis Good

New York, New York

FIX-IT AND FORGET-IT® BAKING WITH YOUR SLOW COOKER

All photographs by Oliver Parini (www.oliverparini.com) except as listed below. Photographs on pages v, ix-xiv, 22, 58, 88, 110-111, 142, 172, 206, 226, 258, 276, and 294 by Jeremy Hess
Recipe food styling by Natalie Wise

Special thanks to JK Adams (www.jkadams.com) for providing cutting boards, cloth napkins, and more, and to Donald and Martha Gehring for use of their home and dishware, tablecloths, and much more, for the photographs in this book.

Good Books books may be purchased in bulk at special discounts for sales promotion, corporate gifts, fund-raising, or educational purposes. Special editions can also be created to specifications. For details, contact the Special Sales Department, Good Books, 307 West 36th Street, 11th Floor, New York, NY 10018 or info@skyhorsepublishing.com.

Good Books in an imprint of Skyhorse Publishing, Inc.®, a Delaware corporation.

Visit our website at www.goodbooks.com.

10 9 8 7 6 5 4 3

Library of Congress Cataloging-in-Publication Data is available on file.
Cover design by Abigail Gehring
Cover photograph by Jeremy Hess
Photographs in text by Oliver Parini

ISBN: 978-1-68099-051-5
Ebook ISBN: 978-1-68099-105-5

Printed in China

Table of Contents

Why Would You Bake in a Slow Cooker?

• A few reasons

It's a blisteringly hot August morning, and I just made a batch of brownies. I never touched my oven.

My grandmothers used to talk about doing their canning in their summer kitchens—a little out-building attached to the main house by a breezeway. They kept all the heat out there, away from the living quarters.

Today I bake in my slow cooker. Same strategy.

Then there are the days when my oven's full, or set at a different temperature than I need to bake my muffins. Out comes my slow cooker.

But there's something more. The breads, the cakes, the pies, the bars turn out with gorgeous crumbs, luscious moistness, splendid flavor. You're not sacrificing when you bake these desserts in your slow cooker.

It takes enormous willpower to develop recipes for a baking book when you can't resist chocolate or fruit pies. Or pizza or from-scratch yeast breads. When I first began, I thought I'd freeze all these good things I was baking and serve them to friends over several weeks, maybe months. Then I admitted what happens when I know there's good stuff in the freezer. I can't go to bed without a small bowlful.

Turns out my daughter was hosting her supper club while I was working on these recipes, and there are some good-sized eaters in the group who can put away a lot of food.

"Mom, I never heard guys talk about crumb structure and moistness before," she said, when she brought back the empty containers. "They kept shaking their heads and wielding their forks over their wedges of cake, talking between bites about how evenly baked and delicious it all was. And the women were back for seconds and thirds, looking guilty but happy!"

• **Planning differently**

Just remember to start your slow-cooker baking a little earlier in the day than when you use your oven.

Most of these recipes need at least an hour and a half, and in many cases more, in the cooker. So you're free to run errands, work in your yard, catch lunch with a friend, or take your kids to music lessons while things bake.

• **Don't miss the wide variety**

Don't get stuck in one section of these baking recipes. Make sure you try the cobblers and crisps, the quiches and granolas, along with the puddings and pies, the yeast and the quick breads.

• **A few things that don't work—or need special attention—in a slow cooker**

I discovered that it doesn't work to crumble a streusel topping over a cake or cupcakes when first putting the batter in to bake. It melts and sinks in. You can add the streusel after the cake is fully baked. Sprinkle it evenly over top, then bake the cake about 20 minutes longer, uncovered. (Do cupcakes for about 10 minutes longer, uncovered.) If you'd like the topping to crisp up and brown, put the cake under the broiler for a minute or two. But watch carefully so you don't burn it.

Nor does a cream cheese middle layer or stuffing keep its identity in cupcakes when you're baking them in a slow cooker. The cream cheese just disappears straight into the batter.

Be careful about increasing the amount of chopped fruit in a cake or quick bread beyond what the recipe calls for. The moisture content in the fruit weighs things down so that the cake or bread won't rise as it should. It will taste good, but it will be gummy—even after 7½ hours on High. I found out.

• **Doing the "Swoop"**

A lot of moisture gathers on the inside of your slow cooker lid whenever you use it. You don't want those drops dripping onto what you've just baked.

So you do the "Swoop" when removing the lid. Grip the handle of the lid firmly, and with a swift and firm move, lift the lid and turn it right-side up in a take-charge single motion.

I hope you enjoy baking with your slow cooker and serving your family and friends from it. Remember, it's a great way to take a dessert or savory baked dish to a potluck or buffet meal— or to bring some real delight to your tailgating party. Or to serve any night or day of the week!

—Phyllis Good

What Size Slow Cookers Should You Have for Baking?

I suggest that you have a **5- or 6-quart round slow cooker, plus a 6-quart oval slow cooker** to start. With those two sizes and shapes, you'll be able to make the recipes in this book.

You can fit a 1-quart round baking dish with a lid, as well as a 2-quart round baking dish with a lid, into your 5- or 6-quart round slow cooker. You can also fit a 6½" or 7" springform pan into either of those round slow cookers.

You can fit four or five 3" (6-oz.) ramekins into a 6-quart oval slow cooker without having them touch each other. You'll use the ramekins for baking muffins, cupcakes, and individual custards.

You can sit a good-sized bread or loaf pan (9¼" x 5¼" x 2¾" or smaller) on the floor of a 6-quart oval slow cooker. Or you can hang it onto the top edge of the oval cooker if it doesn't fit onto the floor of the cooker.

• Other useful equipment to have

1. Oven mitts—You want them to be well insulated but not too thick. You'll wear them to lift the baking dishes, ramekins, and loaf pans out of the slow cooker crock.
   If the baking dish fits fairly tightly into the crock, and if the mitts are too thick, it may be a squeeze to lift out the baking dish.
2. Sturdy tongs—I sometimes use these to lift ramekins out of the hot crock. You need a hefty pair with a bear-jaw grip. And I always have a hot mat in my other hand to support the bottom of whatever I'm lifting out with tongs.
3. Cooling or baking rack—You'll use this all the time when the slow cooker has finished its job. You'll either lift the crock out of the cooker's electrical unit, or you'll lift out the baking dish, loaf pan, or ramekins.

Place the hot container on the cooling rack so air can circulate the whole way around it. This helps keep the baked item from getting soggy and allows it to cool faster.

Might be good to have two of these racks. You can stack one on top of the other if you want to cool a heavy, full crock. Or if you're cooling baking sheets, you'll be glad for the extra space.

REMEMBER, YOUR SLOW COOKER WORKS FOR YOU!

It's capable of a lot more than you might have imagined. So don't be shy about what you ask it to do—like make cakes and breads and breakfast while you sleep.

Or help you cook a meal for guests while you're away enjoying a movie or football game together.

Or relieve pressure when you're hosting the whole family for a holiday meal.

These are near-miracle appliances, especially if you understand a little bit about how they work. Here are a few things I learned along the way.

- ### Let's get rid of two myths right now—

  Myth #1 "Slow cookers are a winter-time appliance." That's just a quarter of the truth. Remember that they can do their quiet slow work without heating up your kitchen in the summertime. And they're just as happy cooking for you while you're at the pool with your kids or working in your lawn or garden. Slow cookers will definitely work for you year-round.

  Myth #2 "The main thing to make in them is beef stew." That's only one-tenth of the truth, maybe less. And this book will prove that to you unmistakably!

- ### A very big point—

  Learn to know your slow cooker. Plan a little get-acquainted time. Each slow cooker has its own personality—just like your oven and your car.

  Plus, many new slow cookers cook hotter and faster than earlier models. I think that with all of the concern for food safety, the slow cooker manufacturers have amped up their settings so that "High," "Low," and "Warm" are all higher temperatures than in the older models. That means they cook hotter—and therefore, faster—than the first slow cookers. The beauty of these little machines is that they're supposed to cook low and slow. We count on that when we flip the switch in the morning before we leave the house for 10 hours or so.

  So—because none of us knows what kind of temperament our slow cooker has until we try it out, nor how hot it cooks—don't assume anything.

Save yourself a disappointment and make the first recipe in your new slow cooker on a day when you're at home. Cook it for the shortest amount of time the recipe calls for. Then check the food to see if it's done. Or if you start smelling food that seems to be finished, turn off the cooker and keep your food from over-cooking.

Then write in your cookbook, next to the recipe you made, exactly how long it took to cook it. The next time you make it, you won't need to try to remember.

And apply what you learned to the next recipes you make in your cooker. If another recipe says it needs to cook 7-9 hours, and you've discovered you own a fast and furious model, cook that recipe for 6-6 ½ hours and then check it. You can always cook a recipe longer. Too bad you can't reverse things if you've overdone it.

Slow-cooked food doesn't have to taste over-cooked. You don't have to sacrifice the cooker's convenience to take care of that.

YOUR SLOW COOKER GUIDEBOOK

• Things you'll be happier knowing!

1. I think it's worth investing in a cooker that allows you to program in the cooking time you want, and then switches to Warm automatically if you're not there to take out the finished dish the moment it stops cooking. You can find reasonably priced cookers that have these functions. And you'll have bought yourself real convenience.

2. Use only the amount of liquid called for in a recipe. In contrast to an oven or a stovetop, a slow cooker tends to draw juices out of food and then harbor it.

3. There are consequences to lifting the lid on your slow cooker while it's cooking. To compensate for the lost heat, you should plan to add 15-20 minutes of cooking time for each time the lid was lifted off.

4. A working slow cooker gets hot on the outside—and I mean the outer electrical unit as well as the inner vessel. Make sure that curious and unsuspecting children or adults don't grab hold of either part. Use oven mitts when lifting any part of a hot cooker, including the lid.

Approximate Slow Cooker Temperatures:
   • High—212°F-300°F (Remember, each slow cooker is different.)
   • Low—170°F-200°F
   • Simmer—185°F
   • Warm—165°F

5. One hour of cooking on High is equal to about 2½ hours of cooking on Low.

Quick Breads

Raspberry Almond Bread

Makes one 9" loaf

Prep. Time: 20 minutes ❦ *Cooking Time: 3–4 hours* ❦ *Standing Time: 20 minutes*
Ideal slow-cooker size: 6-quart

1 cup whole wheat flour

1 cup all-purpose flour

¼ cup rolled oats

⅔ cup sugar

2 tsp. baking powder

1 tsp. baking soda

½ tsp. salt

1 cup fresh *or* unsweetened
frozen raspberries (do not thaw)

½ cup sliced almonds,
lightly toasted

1 egg, lightly beaten

½ cup plain yogurt

⅓ cup canola oil

½ tsp. almond extract

TIP

Wonderful
sliced and
spread with
Nutella.

1. In large bowl, mix flours, oats, sugar, baking powder, baking soda, and salt. Gently stir in raspberries and almonds.

2. Separately, mix egg, yogurt, oil, and almond extract.

3. Gently stir wet ingredients into dry until just barely mixed—streaks of flour are fine.

4. Pour batter into greased and floured loaf pan that fits in your slow cooker.

5. Place pan of batter into crock on jar lid or metal trivet. Cover and place wooden chopstick or spoon handle under lid to vent at one end.

6. Cook on High for 3–4 hours, until edges of bread are pulling away from sides and tester inserted in middle of loaf comes out clean. Bread does not brown as much as oven-baked bread!

7. Wearing oven mitts to protect your knuckles, remove hot pan from cooker.

8. Allow bread to cool 10 minutes. Run a knife around the edge, and turn loaf out onto cooling rack for 10 more minutes before slicing. Serve warm.

Banana Peanut Butter Bread

Makes one 9" loaf

Prep. Time: 20 minutes ❦ Cooking Time: 3–4 hours ❦ Standing Time: 10 minutes
Ideal slow-cooker size: 6-quart

1 cup all-purpose flour

1 cup whole wheat flour

1 tsp. baking soda

½ tsp. salt

1 cup mashed ripe banana (about 2 medium)

½ cup creamy peanut butter

½ cup sugar

⅓ cup plain yogurt

⅓ cup vegetable oil

2 eggs

1 tsp. vanilla extract

1 cup semisweet chocolate chips

1. In a mixing bowl, combine flours, baking soda, and salt.

2. Separately, mix banana, peanut butter, sugar, yogurt, oil, eggs, and vanilla. When thoroughly mixed, stir in chocolate chips.

3. Add wet ingredients to dry ingredients, stirring just until combined.

4. Pour batter in greased and floured loaf pan.

5. Set pan on jar lid or metal trivet in slow cooker. Place lid on slow cooker, venting at one end with a wooden spoon handle or chopstick.

6. Cook on High for 3–4 hours, until edges of bread are pulling away from sides and tester inserted in middle of loaf comes out clean. Bread will not brown as much as oven-baked bread!

7. Wearing oven gloves to protect your knuckles, remove hot pan from cooker and allow to cool 10 minutes. Run a knife around the loaf and turn it out onto cooling rack. Slices best when cool, if you can wait that long!

Why I like this recipe—

This is the trifecta of deliciousness, I think: chocolate, peanut butter, and banana. I serve this bread for breakfast, snacks, or dessert—it's always welcome!

Glazed Poppyseed Bread

Makes one 9" loaf

Prep. Time: 20 minutes   ❦   Cooking Time: 3–4 hours   ❦   Standing Time: 30 minutes

Ideal slow-cooker size: 6-quart

2 cups all-purpose flour

½ cup sugar

½ tsp. salt

1 tsp. baking powder

½ tsp. baking soda

2 Tbsp. poppy seeds

⅓ cup vegetable oil

¼ cup buttermilk

1 egg

juice and zest of 1 lemon

Glaze:

1 cup confectioners sugar

¼ tsp. butter extract

¼ tsp. almond extract

pinch salt

2–3 Tbsp. milk

1. In a mixing bowl, combine flour, sugar, salt, baking powder, baking soda, and poppy seeds.

2. Separately, mix oil, egg, lemon zest, and lemon juice.

3. Add wet ingredients to flour mixture and mix just until combined.

4. Pour batter into greased and floured loaf pan that fits in your slow cooker.

5. Place pan of batter into crock on jar lid or metal trivet. Cover and place wooden chopstick or spoon handle under lid to vent at one end.

6. Cook on High for 3–4 hours, until edges of bread are pulling away from sides and tester inserted in middle of loaf comes out clean. Bread will not brown as much as oven-baked bread!

7. Wearing oven mitts to protect your knuckles, remove hot pan from cooker.

8. Allow bread to cool 10 minutes while you make the glaze.

9. To make glaze, combine ingredients in small bowl, using lesser amount of milk. Add more milk as needed to make thick, pourable glaze.

10. Run a knife around edge of loaf and turn out onto cooling rack.

11. Poke holes in top of loaf with a skewer or chopstick. Pour glaze slowly and evenly over top of loaf. Allow to rest for 10–20 minutes before slicing.

A great variation—

The glaze is optional—the bread will still be delicious and moist without it.

Strawberries and Cream Bread

Makes one 9" loaf

Prep. Time: 30 minutes ❦ *Cooking Time: 3–4 hours* ❦ *Standing Time: 20 minutes*
Ideal slow-cooker size: 6-quart

1 ½ cup diced strawberries

2 tsp. lemon juice

2 cups all-purpose flour

1 cup sugar

½ tsp. salt

2 tsp. baking powder

½ cup vegetable oil

½ cup orange juice

1 ½ tsp. vanilla

1 egg

8 oz. pkg. cream cheese, room temperature, diced

TIP

Sprinkle loaf with confectioners sugar before serving.

1. In a small bowl, combine strawberries and lemon juice. Set aside.

2. In a mixing bowl, combine flour, sugar, salt, and baking powder.

3. Separately, combine oil, orange juice, vanilla, and egg. Whisk. Stir in cream cheese.

4. Add strawberries to oil mixture.

5. Combine wet and dry mixtures, stirring gently just until combined.

6. Pour batter in greased and floured loaf pan that fits in your slow cooker.

7. Set pan on jar lid or metal trivet in slow cooker. Place lid on slow cooker, venting at one end with a wooden spoon handle or chopstick.

8. Cook on High for 3–4 hours, until edges of bread are pulling away from sides and tester inserted in middle of loaf comes out clean. Bread will not brown as much as oven-baked bread!

9. Wearing oven gloves to protect your knuckles, remove hot pan from cooker and allow to cool 10 minutes. Run a knife around the loaf and turn it out onto cooling rack. Wait 10 more minutes before slicing.

Rosemary Raisin Bread

Makes one 9" loaf

Prep. Time: 20 minutes   ❧   Cooking Time: 3–4 hours   ❧   Standing Time: 20 minutes
Ideal slow-cooker size: 6-quart

1¼ cups whole wheat flour
1¼ cups all-purpose flour
½ cup sugar
½ tsp. baking soda
½ tsp. baking powder
½ tsp. salt
1½ tsp. dried rosemary
1 cup raisins
1½ cups buttermilk

Some great variations—

1. Substitute 1 cup plain yogurt mixed with ½ cup milk for the buttermilk. 2. May substitute more all-purpose flour for the whole wheat flour. 3. This bread is lovely toasted and then spread with butter or lemon curd.

1. In a mixing bowl, combine flours, sugar, baking soda, baking powder, salt, and rosemary. Stir in raisins.

2. Add buttermilk and mix gently, just until combined.

3. Pour batter into greased and floured loaf pan that fits in your slow cooker.

4. Place pan of batter into crock on jar lid or metal trivet. Cover and place wooden chopstick or spoon handle under lid to vent at one end.

5. Cook on High for 3–4 hours, until edges of bread are pulling away from sides and tester inserted in middle of loaf comes out clean. Bread will not brown as much as oven-baked bread!

6. Wearing oven mitts to protect your knuckles, remove hot pan from cooker.

7. Allow bread to cool 10 minutes. Run a knife around the edge, and turn loaf out onto cooling rack for 10 more minutes before slicing. Serve warm.

Thanksgiving Bread

Makes one 9" loaf

Prep. Time: 30 minutes ❧ Cooking Time: 3–4 hours ❧ Standing Time: 10 minutes
Ideal slow-cooker size: 6-quart

1¾ cups flour

¼ cup stone-ground cornmeal

¾ cup sugar

1½ tsp. baking powder

½ tsp. salt

⅓ cup oil

1 Tbsp. grated orange zest

½ cup orange juice

1 egg

1 cup chopped fresh cranberries

½ cup chopped walnuts

1. In a mixing bowl, combine flour, cornmeal, sugar, baking powder, and salt.

2. Separately, mix oil, zest, juice, and egg. Beat. Stir in cranberries and walnuts.

3. Add wet ingredients to dry ingredients, stirring just until combined.

4. Pour batter in greased and floured loaf pan.

5. Set pan on jar lid or metal trivet in slow cooker. Place lid on slow cooker, venting at one end with a wooden spoon handle or chopstick.

6. Cook on High for 3–4 hours, until edges of bread are pulling away from sides and tester inserted in middle of loaf comes out clean. Bread will not brown as much as oven-baked bread!

7. Wearing oven gloves to protect your knuckles, remove hot pan from cooker and allow to cool 10 minutes. Run a knife around the loaf and turn it out onto cooling rack. Slices best when cool, if you can wait that long!

TIP

You may substitute more all-purpose flour for the whole wheat flour.

Why I like this recipe—

These are the flavors of autumn, especially that little surprise hit of corn from the cornmeal. I love to make this bread sometime close to Thanksgiving when the fresh cranberries start appearing in the stores. I also buy a few extra bags of cranberries and stash them in the freezer for later—just thaw a cup, drain well, and chop.

Irish Oatmeal Bread

Makes one 9" loaf

Prep. Time: 25 minutes   ❧   Cooking Time: 3–4 hours   ❧   Standing Time: 6–10 hours
Ideal slow-cooker size: 6-quart

1 cup plain full-fat yogurt
⅔ cup milk
1 cup rolled oats
2 eggs
2 Tbsp. oil
¾ cup dark brown sugar
1 cup whole wheat flour
⅔ cup all-purpose flour
1 tsp. baking soda
1 tsp. salt

1. Combine yogurt, milk, and oats in bowl with lid. Refrigerate for 6–10 hours.

2. Add eggs, oil, and sugar to yogurt mixture. Mix well.

3. Separately, combine both flours, baking soda, and salt.

4. Stir flour mixture gently into yogurt mixture.

5. Pour batter into greased and floured loaf pan that fits into cooker.

6. Set loaf pan on a jar lid or trivet on the floor of the cooker. Prop lid open at one end with a wooden spoon handle or chopstick.

7. Cook on High for 3–4 hours, until edges of bread are pulling away from sides and tester inserted in middle of loaf comes out clean. Bread will not brown as much as oven-baked bread!

8. Wearing oven gloves to protect your knuckles, remove hot pan from hot cooker. Allow to cool 10 minutes. Run a knife around the loaf and turn loaf out onto a cooling rack to finish cooling. Slices most easily when cool if you can wait that long.

TIP

The overnight soak gives a delicious flavor and texture to the bread; it's surprisingly light for its hearty ingredients. I serve it with butter, marmalade, or mild cheese.

Little Boston Brown Loaves

Makes four 16-oz. loaves

Prep. Time: 30 minutes ❦ Cooking Time: 5–6 hours

Ideal slow-cooker size: 6-quart

1 cup whole wheat flour

½ cup stone-ground cornmeal

½ cup rye flour

2 tsp. baking soda

1 tsp. salt

¼ tsp. allspice

¾ cup chopped raisins

1½ cups buttermilk

½ cup blackstrap molasses

2 Tbsp. butter, room temperature

1. In a mixing bowl, combine flours, cornmeal, baking soda, salt, and allspice. Stir in raisins.

2. Separately, mix buttermilk and molasses.

3. Add buttermilk mixture to flour mixture. Stir until just combined. Set aside while you prepare the cans and cooker.

4. Use 4 clean 15- or 16-oz. cans. Grease insides generously with butter.

5. Divide batter between the 4 cans to fill cans ⅔ full. Grease squares of tin foil with butter and use to make tight lids on each can.

6. Set cans in slow cooker. Pour in water to come halfway up the sides of the cans.

7. Cover and cook on Low for 5–6 hours, until skewer inserted through foil lid into bread comes out clean.

8. Carefully remove hot cans (a jar lifter is helpful), uncover, and allow to rest for 10 minutes. Run a knife around the edge of each loaf and turn loaves out onto cooling rack to cool. Slices easily when cool if you can wait that long.

TIP

Serve with a traditional New England supper of baked beans, or eat as breakfast toast with cream cheese.

Buttery Beer Bread

Makes one 9" loaf

Prep. Time: 15 minutes ❦ *Cooking Time: 3–4 hours* ❦ *Standing Time: 20 minutes*
Ideal slow-cooker size: 6-quart

1 cup whole wheat flour

2 cups all-purpose flour

2 Tbsp. sugar

3 tsp. baking powder

1 tsp. salt

12-oz. beer, any kind, room temperature

¼ cup melted butter

1. In a mixing bowl, combine flours, sugar, baking powder, and salt.

2. Add beer and mix.

3. Pour batter in greased and floured loaf pan that fits in your slow cooker. Drizzle top of loaf with melted butter.

4. Set pan on jar lid or metal trivet in slow cooker. Place lid on slow cooker, venting at one end with a wooden spoon handle or chopstick.

5. Cook on High for 3–4 hours, until edges of bread are pulling away from sides and tester inserted in middle of loaf comes out clean. Bread will not brown as much as oven-baked bread!

6. Wearing oven gloves to protect your knuckles, remove hot pan from cooker and allow to cool 10 minutes. Run a knife around the loaf and turn it out onto cooling rack, waiting 10 more minutes for easiest slicing.

Why I like this recipe—
I love having this savory bread on hand for soup meals in the winter. It's less fuss than yeast bread, but seems extra-special with its buttery top.

Just Cornbread

Makes 4–6 servings
Prep. Time: 20 minutes ❦ *Cooking Time: 2–3 hours*
Ideal slow-cooker size: 6-quart

1 cup all-purpose flour

1 cup stone-ground yellow cornmeal

4 tsp. baking powder

1 tsp. salt

2 Tbsp. brown sugar

1 egg

1 cup milk

⅓ cup oil

1 Tbsp. butter

TIP

You may also put the batter in a loaf pan and bake per directions given with Buttery Beer Bread on page 19.

1. In a mixing bowl, combine flour, cornmeal, baking powder, salt, and brown sugar.

2. Make a well in the dry ingredients. Add egg, milk, and oil.

3. Whisk wet ingredients lightly, drawing in the dry ingredients until ingredients are just mixed with streaks of flour remaining.

4. Grease slow cooker with butter.

5. Pour batter in slow cooker. Smooth top.

6. Cover. Cook on High for 2–3 hours until edges are pulling away from the sides and tester inserted in middle comes out clean. Bread will not brown as much as oven-baked bread!

Some great variations—

If you want more than just cornbread: 1. Add ½ cup grated sharp cheese, 1 tsp. paprika, and ½ tsp. dried oregano for Cheesy Cornbread. 2. Add ¼ cup chopped fresh cilantro, ½ cup corn, ½ tsp. chili powder, and 4-oz. can green chilies, well-drained, for Mexican Cornbread. 3. Replace part of the oil with bacon drippings, replace the brown sugar with ¼ cup maple syrup and reduce milk to ¾ cup, and add ¼ tsp. baking soda. Sprinkle top of batter with chopped, cooked bacon bits. This is Maple-Bacon Cornbread.

Muffins
and
Cupcakes

Graham Cracker Cupcakes

Makes 4 large cupcakes

Prep. Time: 15–20 minutes ❧ Cooking Time: 2 hours ❧ Standing Time: 1 day
Ideal slow-cooker size: 6- or 7-quart oval

I Tbsp. shortening

¼ cup sugar

I small egg

8 graham crackers, crushed

½ tsp. baking powder

¼ cup chopped nuts of your choice, *optional*

¼ tsp. vanilla

¼ cup milk

¼ cup unsweetened crushed pineapple

¼ cup sugar

1. Beat shortening and sugar together until creamy.

2. Beat in egg, crushed graham crackers, baking powder, nuts if you wish, vanilla, and milk. Mix well.

3. Grease interior of four 3-oz. ramekins. Divide batter among them.

4. Place filled ramekins into slow cooker crock. Cover with slow cooker lid.

5. Bake on High 2 hours, or until tester inserted in center of ramekins comes out clean.

6. While cupcakes are baking, cook unsweetened pineapple and sugar together for a few minutes, until sugar melts.

7. Spoon mixture over tops of baked cupcakes. Allow to stand, covered, for at least a day before serving.

Why I like this recipe—
If you still feel warm about graham crackers from when you were a kid, here's a tasty twist on them, kept moist by the pineapple surprise.

Pumpkin Coconut Cupcakes

Makes 4 large cupcakes
Prep. Time: 20 minutes ❦ Cooking Time: 2–3 hours
Ideal slow-cooker size: 6- or 7-quart oval

½ cup sugar

½ cup cooked *or* canned pumpkin

⅓ cup cooking oil

1 egg

½ cup flour

¼ tsp. salt

½ tsp. baking powder

½ tsp. baking soda

½ tsp. cinnamon

dash of nutmeg

2 Tbsp. unsweetened grated coconut

cinnamon and sugar

1. Mix together ½ cup sugar, pumpkin, oil, and egg.

2. In a separate bowl, mix together flour, salt, baking powder, baking soda, cinnamon, and nutmeg. Pour into wet ingredients and mix well.

3. Fold in coconut.

4. Grease interior of four ramekins.

5. Divide batter among them. Place in slow cooker crock.

6. Sprinkle each filled ramekin with a light dusting of cinnamon and sugar.

7. Cover crock with slow cooker lid.

8. Bake on High 2 hours, or until tester inserted in center of ramekins comes out clean.

9. Pull on oven mitts to lift ramekins out of crock, or use a sturdy set of tongs. Place ramekins on wire baking rack to cool.

TIP

If you open a can of pumpkin to make these, put what's left in a freezable container, and mark the amount that remains on top. Then you can make another batch of Pumpkin Coconut Cupcakes whenever you get the inspiration. Btw, grated coconut freezes well, too.

Fresh Peach Cupcakes

Makes 4 large cupcakes
Prep. Time: 20 minutes   ❦   Cooking Time: 2 hours
Ideal slow-cooker size: 6- or 7-quart oval

5⅓ Tbsp. (⅓ stick) butter, softened

⅔ cup sugar

1 large egg

⅔ cup flour

⅔ tsp. baking powder

1 Tbsp. + 1 tsp. sour cream

⅔ tsp. vanilla

2–3 fresh peaches, peeled and sliced

⅓ tsp. cinnamon

⅓ tsp. sugar

1. Cream butter and ⅔ cup sugar until light and fluffy.

2. Beat in egg.

3. In a separate bowl, stir together flour and baking powder. Add dry ingredients to wet, stirring just until mixed.

4. Stir in sour cream and vanilla, again stirring until just mixed.

5. Grease interior of four 3-oz. ramekins. Divide batter among ramekins.

6. Top ramekins with sliced peaches. Then sprinkle each ramekin with cinnamon and sugar.

7. Place filled ramekins into slow cooker crock. Cover with cooker lid.

8. Bake on Low 2 hours, or until tester inserted into center of ramekins comes out clean.

9. Put on oven mitts and lift ramekins out of crock, or use a pair of sturdy tongs. Place on wire baking rack to cool.

Why I like this recipe—
    These are soft and moist and light, almost like mini peach cobblers.

Pineapple Zucchini Cupcakes

Makes 4 large cupcakes
Prep. Time: 20–30 minutes ❧ Cooking Time: 2–3 hours
Ideal slow-cooker size: 6- or 7-quart oval

1 small egg

½ cup sugar

½ tsp. vanilla

¼ cup cooking oil

½ cup grated zucchini

¾ cup flour

¼ tsp. baking powder

¼ tsp. baking soda

¼ tsp. salt

2 Tbsp. crushed pineapple, undrained

¼ cup raisins

¼ cup nuts of your choice

Creamy Frosting:

2 Tbsp. Greek yogurt

2 Tbsp. butter, softened

½–¾ cup confectioners sugar, sifted

1. In a good-sized bowl, beat egg, sugar, vanilla, and cooking oil together until fluffy.

2. Stir in grated zucchini, flour, baking powder, baking soda, and salt, mixing well.

3. Stir in crushed pineapple, raisins, and nuts, mixing well.

4. Grease interior of four 3-oz. ramekins. Divide cupcake batter among the four.

5. Place ramekins into slow cooker crock. Cover with slow cooker lid.

6. Bake on Low 2–3 hours, or until tester inserted in center of ramekins comes out clean.

7. Lift the ramekins out carefully, using oven mitts to protect your knuckles, or using sturdy tongs. Place on a wire baking rack to cool before frosting.

8. While cupcakes cool, mix frosting ingredients together. Frost when cupcakes are completely cool.

Why I like this recipe—

Here's what the tester said: These are wonderful and moist. I added 3/4 tsp. pumpkin spice to one batch I made, and we preferred those above the plain ones. Whichever way you decide to make them, this is one great way to include zucchini in a dish!

Double Chocolate Muffins

Makes 4 large muffins

Prep. Time: 20–30 minutes ❦ *Cooking Time: 2–3 hours*

Ideal slow-cooker size: 6- or 7-quart oval

¼ cup dry quick oats

2¾ Tbsp. milk

½ cup all-purpose flour

¼ cup whole wheat flour

1 Tbsp. wheat *or* oat bran

¼ cup sugar

2 Tbsp. brown sugar

2¾ Tbsp. unsweetened cocoa powder

⅛ tsp. salt

rounded ½ tsp. baking powder

1 small egg

2 Tbsp. vegetable oil

½ cup milk

1½ tsp. vanilla

⅓ cup chocolate chips

Glaze:

½–1 Tbsp. peanut butter, creamy *or* crunchy

¾ cup confectioners sugar

tiny bit of water

1. In a microwave-safe container, combine quick oats and 2¾ Tbsp. milk. Microwave on High 1 minute. Set aside.

2. In a good-sized bowl, combine flours, bran, sugars, cocoa powder, salt, and baking powder.

3. To the bowl with the oats mixture, add the egg, oil, ½ cup milk, vanilla, and chocolate chips.

4. Gently add wet ingredients to dry, mixing just until moistened.

5. Grease interior of four 3-oz. ramekins. Divide batter equally among them.

6. Place ramekins into slow cooker crock. Cover with slow cooker lid.

7. Bake on High 2 hours, or until tester inserted into center of ramekins comes out clean.

8. Pull on oven mitts and lift ramekins out of cooker and onto wire baking rack to cool. Or use a sturdy pair of tongs to lift them out.

9. When the muffins are cooled, make the glaze. Combine peanut butter and confectioners sugar in a bowl. Stir together gently. When well mixed, stir in a tsp. of water. You want to drizzle the glaze, so add only a little bit of water at a time, until you can drizzle it onto the muffins without it sliding it off to the edges.

Why I like this recipe—

Good texture, deep down chocolate flavor, light on calories—what more can you ask for from a muffin? Oh, and the peanut butter, too.

Pecan Muffins

Makes 4 large muffins
Prep. Time: 15 minutes 🌱 *Cooking Time: 1½–2 hours*
Ideal slow-cooker size: 6- or 7-quart oval

½ cup brown sugar
¼ cup flour
½ cup chopped pecans
⅓ cup melted butter
I egg

1. Combine brown sugar, flour, and pecans in a good-sized mixing bowl.

2. In a separate smaller bowl, combine butter and egg.

3. Stir wet ingredients into dry, just until moistened.

4. Grease interior of four 3-oz. ramekins. Divide batter evenly among the ramekins.

5. Place filled ramekins into slow cooker crock. Cover with slow cooker lid.

6. Bake on High 1½–2 hours, or until tester inserted into center of ramekins comes out clean.

7. Wearing oven mitts, lift out ramekins and place on wire baking rack to cool. Or use a sturdy pair of tongs to lift them out.

8. Serve warm or at room temperature.

TIP
These freeze well and thaw in a minute or less in the microwave.

Morning Glory Muffins

Makes 4 large muffins
Prep. Time: 20–30 minutes   ❧   Cooking Time: 2–3 hours
Ideal slow-cooker size: 6– or 7– quart oval

1 small egg

¼ cup vegetable oil

½ tsp. vanilla

scant ⅓ cup sugar

½ cup + 1 ½ tsp. flour

½ tsp. baking soda

½ tsp. cinnamon

⅛ tsp. salt

½ cup grated carrots

¼ cup raisins

2 Tbsp. chopped nuts of your choice

2 Tbsp. grated unsweetened coconut

¼ apple, peeled and grated *or* finely chopped

1. In a good-sized mixing bowl, beat egg. Then add oil, vanilla, and sugar and combine well.

2. In a separate mixing bowl, stir together flour, baking soda, cinnamon, and salt. When well mixed, add grated carrots, raisins, chopped nuts, grated coconut, and grated or chopped apple. Stir together well.

3. Add dry ingredients mixed with fruit and nuts into creamed ingredients. Blend just until everything is moistened.

4. Grease interior of four 3-oz. ramekins. Divide batter equally among the ramekins.

5. Place ramekins into slow cooker crock. Cover with slow cooker lid.

6. Bake on Low 2–3 hours, or until tester inserted into center of ramekins comes out clean.

7. Put on oven mitts and lift ramekins onto wire baking rack to cool. Or use a sturdy pair of tongs to lift them out.

8. Serve warm or at room temperature.

Why I like this recipe—

These muffins have a great texture. And because there are so many different ingredients, the texture's different with every bite. They remind me of carrot cake without the icing, and they certainly don't need it. Add a dab of cream cheese or butter if you want.

Light Banana Raisin Muffins

Makes 4 large muffins

Prep. Time: 20 minutes   ❦   Cooking Time: 2–3 hours

Ideal slow-cooker size: 6- or 7-quart oval

⅓ cup flour

⅓ cup dry rolled oats

1 tsp. baking powder

rounded ¼ tsp. cinnamon

⅓ cup skim milk

⅓ cup smooshed ripe bananas

⅓ cup raisins

1 Tbsp. + 1 tsp. vegetable oil

1 Tbsp. + 1 tsp. brown sugar, packed

small egg white

1. Combine flour, dry oats, baking powder, and cinnamon in a good-sized bowl. Set aside.

2. Combine remaining ingredients in a separate bowl until well mixed.

3. Add wet ingredients to dry, mixing just until dry ingredients are moistened.

4. Grease interior of four 3-oz. ramekins. Divide batter among ramekins.

5. Place filled ramekins into slow cooker crock. Cover with slow cooker lid.

6. Bake on High 2 hours, or until tester inserted into center of ramekins comes out clean.

7. Wearing oven mitts, lift ramekins out of cooker and place on wire baking rack to cool. Or use a sturdy pair of tongs to do the lifting.

8. Serve warm or at room temperature.

TIP

These are a quick and easy breakfast. And they're a good way to use a ripe banana! The sugar content is low (remember— "Light"), so bring out some marmalade for those who like a little more sweetness.

Banana Grove Cupcakes

Makes 4 large cupcakes
Prep. Time: 20–30 minutes ❧ Cooking Time: 2–3 hours
Ideal slow-cooker size: 6- or 7-quart oval

1⅔ Tbsp. shortening

⅓ cup sugar

I small egg

¼ tsp. vanilla

¼ cup ripe smooshed bananas

½ cup flour

dash of salt

scant ¼ tsp. baking powder

¾ Tbsp. sour milk*

pinch of baking soda

*If you don't have sour milk, put a few drops lemon juice *or* vinegar in Tbsp. Fill Tbsp. with milk. Allow to stand for 2–3 minutes before adding to batter.

1. Beat shortening and sugar together until creamed.

2. Add egg, vanilla, and smooshed bananas. Mix together well.

3. In a separate bowl, stir together flour, salt, and baking powder.

4. In a small additional bowl, mix sour milk and baking soda.

5. Add flour mixture and sour milk mixture alternately to shortening mixture. Mix thoroughly.

6. Grease interior of four ramekins.

7. Divide batter among four ramekins, and then place into slow cooker crock.

8. Cover with slow cooker lid.

9. Bake on High 2 hours, or until tester inserted in center of ramekins comes out clean.

10. Put on baking mitts to lift out the ramekins, or use a sturdy pair of tongs. Place on wire baking rack to cool.

11. These are soooo good with peanut butter icing and a few chopped walnuts.

TIP

All you need is one very ripe banana— and you've got a sweet and tender breakfast or soup go-along.

Raspberry Streusel Muffins

Makes 4 large muffins
Prep. Time: 20–30 minutes ❦ Cooking Time: 2–3 hours
Ideal slow-cooker size: 6- or 7-quart oval

4 Tbsp. (half a stick) butter, softened

¼ cup sugar

small egg

1 cup flour

¼ tsp. baking soda

¼ tsp. baking powder

¼ tsp. cinnamon

⅛ tsp. salt

¼ cup milk

¼ cup sour cream

½ tsp. vanilla

½ cup raspberries, black *or* red

confectioners sugar

Topping:

¼ cup flour

¼ cup quick oats

2 Tbsp. + 1 tsp. sugar

¼ tsp. cinnamon

dash of salt

3 Tbsp. butter, softened

1. Beat butter and sugar together in good-sized bowl until light and creamy. Add egg and beat until well blended.

2. In a separate bowl, combine flour, baking soda, baking powder, cinnamon, and salt.

3. In another bowl, combine milk, sour cream, and vanilla.

4. Add flour mixture to butter-sugar-egg mixture, alternating with milk mixture. Fold mixtures together gently, until ingredients are just combined.

5. Carefully fold in raspberries so as not to damage the berries or over-mix the batter.

6. In the dry bowl you've used, mix together the dry topping ingredients—flour, quick oats, sugar, cinnamon, and salt.

7. When well mixed, work in the butter with your fingers until mixture is crumbly.

8. Grease interior of four 3-oz. ramekins. Divide muffin batter equally among the ramekins. Sprinkle tops with topping. (If you have any streusel topping left over, freeze it for future use.)

9. Place filled ramekins into slow cooker crock. Cover with slow cooker lid.

10. Bake on Low 2–3 hours, or until tester inserted into centers of ramekins comes out clean.

A great variation—

The season for fresh raspberries is so short that sometimes I completely miss it. Then I use frozen raspberries to make these muffins. If you do that, don't thaw the raspberries. Just toss the still frozen berries in a separate bowl with a Tbsp. of flour, right before folding them into the batter.

11. Wearing oven mitts, lift ramekins out of crock and place on wire baking rack to cool. Or use a pair of sturdy tongs to lift out the ramekins.

12. When the muffins are completely cool, sprinkle with confectioners sugar.

Blueberry Oat Muffins

Makes 4 large muffins

Prep. Time: 20 minutes ❦ Cooking Time: 2–3 hours

Ideal slow-cooker size: 6- or 7-quart oval

⅓ cup uncooked rolled oats

⅓ cup schmierkase or buttermilk*

⅓ cup flour

⅓ tsp. baking powder

rounded ¼ tsp. baking soda

¼ tsp. salt

¼ cup brown sugar, lightly packed

1⅓ Tbsp. vegetable oil *or* butter, melted

1 small egg

⅓ cup fresh *or* frozen blueberries

*If you don't have schmierkase *or* buttermilk, place 1 tsp. lemon juice *or* vinegar in ⅓ cup measure. Fill cup with milk. Let stand for 3–4 minutes. Stir, then add to batter.

1. Combine oats and schmierkase or buttermilk in a good-sized bowl.

2. In another bowl, combine flour, baking powder, baking soda, salt, and brown sugar. Stir, blending well.

3. Add oil or butter and egg to oat mixture. Mix well.

4. Add dry ingredients to oat mixture. Stir just until ingredients are moistened.

5. Gently fold in blueberries.

6. Grease interior of four 3-oz. ramekins. Divide batter evenly among ramekins.

7. Place ramekins into slow cooker crock. Cover with slow cooker lid.

8. Bake on High 2 hours, or until tester inserted into center of ramekins comes out clean.

9. Pull on oven mitts and lift ramekins onto wire baking rack to cool. Or use a sturdy pair of tongs.

10. Serve warm or at room temperature.

A great variation—

You can substitute ⅓ cup chopped apples (no need to peel them), plus 1 tsp. cinnamon, for blueberries.

TIP

I like to make these ahead of time and freeze them. Take them out of the freezer and heat them in the microwave before serving.

Apple Pumpkin Muffins

Makes 4 large muffins

Prep. Time: 20–30 minutes ❧ Cooking Time: 2–3 hours
Ideal slow-cooker size: 6- or 7-quart oval

½ cup + 2 Tbsp. flour

½ cup sugar

¾ tsp. pumpkin pie spice

¼ tsp. baking soda

⅛ tsp. salt

1 small egg

¼ cup canned *or* cooked pumpkin

2 Tbsp. vegetable oil

½ cup finely chopped unpeeled apples

Streusel:

1¾ Tbsp. sugar

¾ tsp. flour

⅛ tsp. cinnamon

1 tsp. butter, softened

1. In a good-sized mixing bowl, combine flour, sugar, pumpkin pie spice, baking soda, and salt.

2. In a separate bowl, combine egg, pumpkin, and oil. Stir into dry ingredients, just until moistened.

3. Fold in apples.

4. Grease interior of four 3-oz. ramekins.

5. Divide batter among four ramekins.

6. In a small bowl, combine sugar, flour, and cinnamon for streusel topping. Work in butter with your fingers until mixture becomes crumbly. Sprinkle evenly over tops of filled ramekins.

7. Place ramekins in slow cooker crock. Cover with slow cooker lid.

8. Bake on High 2 hours, or until tester inserted into center of ramekins comes out clean.

9. Put on oven mitts to lift ramekins out of cooker and onto wire baking rack to cool. Or use a sturdy pair of tongs to lift them out.

10. Let cool to warm or room temperature before serving.

TIP

I used to peel apples whenever they went into a recipe, until a friend gave me her recipe for Apple Muffins, which I loved. I had no idea that the apples weren't peeled before going into the batter. That was the end of my peeling apples for most apple dishes I make (except apple pie, but one of these days I'm going to use unpeeled apples in a pie and see what happens)!

Apple Cranberry Muffins

Makes 4 large muffins

Prep. Time: 20 minutes   ❦   Cooking Time: 2–3 hours
Ideal slow-cooker size: 6- or 7-quart oval

½ cup + 1¼ Tbsp. flour

1 Tbsp. + 1 tsp. sugar

rounded ¾ tsp. baking powder

¼ tsp. salt

rounded ⅛ tsp. cinnamon

1 small egg

¼ cup milk

1¾ Tbsp. vegetable oil

⅓ cup apple, unpeeled and finely chopped

3 Tbsp. chopped fresh *or* frozen cranberries

1. In a good-sized mixing bowl, stir together flour, sugar, baking powder, salt, and cinnamon. When well mixed, make a well in the center of the dry ingredients.

2. In a separate bowl, blend together egg, milk, oil, apples, and cranberries.

3. Add wet ingredients all at once to dry. Stir just until moistened.

4. Grease interior of four 3-oz. ramekins.

5. Divide batter equally among four ramekins.

6. Place filled ramekins into slow cooker crock. Cover with slow cooker lid.

7. Bake on High for 2 hours, or until tester inserted into center of ramekins comes out clean.

8. Wearing oven mitts, lift ramekins out of cooker and onto wire baking rack to cool. Or use a sturdy pair of tongs to lift them out.

A great variation—

If I don't have fresh or frozen cranberries, or if I want a little different flavor and texture, I use 3 Tbsp. dried cranberries. They work well and add good flavor.

TIP

Choose a tart baking apple for the best flavor.

Lemon Nut Muffins

Makes 4 large muffins

Prep. Time: 20–30 minutes ❦ Cooking Time: 2–3 hours

Ideal slow-cooker size: 6- or 7-quart oval

¾ cup + 2 Tbsp. flour

½ cup chopped walnuts

2¾ Tbsp. sugar

1 tsp. baking powder

½ tsp. lemon zest

¼ tsp. salt

small egg

¼ cup milk

2¾ Tbsp. butter, melted

2 Tbsp. sour cream

Streusel Topping:

1½ Tbsp. flour

1½ Tbsp. brown sugar

1½ Tbsp. wheat germ, toasted *or* not

1 Tbsp. butter, softened

½ tsp. lemon zest

1. Mix flour, chopped walnuts, sugar, baking powder, lemon zest, and salt together in a good-sized bowl.

2. In a smaller bowl, beat egg with fork. Stir in milk, butter, and sour cream.

3. Stir wet ingredients into dry, just until blended.

4. Grease interior of four 3-oz. ramekins. Divide batter evenly among the four ramekins.

5. Place filled ramekins into slow cooker crock.

6. Prepare streusel topping by combining flour, brown sugar, and wheat germ in bowl. Using your fingers, work in butter and lemon zest until mixture is crumbly.

7. Scatter topping evenly over filled ramekins.

8. Cover crock with slow cooker lid.

9. Bake on High 2 hours, or until tester inserted into center of ramekins comes out clean.

10. Put on oven mitts and lift ramekins out of crock. Place them on a wire baking rack to cool. Or use sturdy tongs to lift out ramekins.

11. Serve warm or at room temperature.

TIP

It won't hurt to up the amount of lemon zest in both the batter and the topping. I love the play between sweet and sour in both parts of these muffins.

Tasty, Crunchy Bran Muffins

Makes 4 large muffins
Prep. Time: 15–20 minutes   ❦   Cooking Time: 2–3 hours
Ideal slow-cooker size: 6- or 7-quart oval

⅓ cup all-bran cereal

2 Tbsp. + 2 tsp. whole wheat flour

2 Tbsp. + 2 tsp. wheat germ, toasted *or* not

2 Tbsp. + 2 tsp. sunflower seeds

⅓ cup raisins

1 tsp. baking powder

1 small egg

⅓ cup milk

1¾ Tbsp. vegetable oil

2 tsp. molasses

⅓ tsp. vanilla

1. Combine dry cereal, flour, wheat germ, sunflower seeds, raisins, and baking powder in a good-sized bowl, mixing well.

2. In a separate bowl, combine egg, milk, vegetable oil, molasses, and vanilla until well mixed.

3. Pour wet ingredients over dry. Mix only until moistened throughout.

4. Grease interior of four 3-oz. ramekins. Divide batter among ramekins.

5. Place ramekins into slow cooker crock. Cover with slow cooker lid.

6. Bake on High 2 hours, or until tester inserted into center of ramekins comes out clean.

7. Wearing oven mitts, lift out ramekins and place on wire baking rack to cool. Or use a pair of sturdy tongs to lift them out.

8. Serve warm or at room temperature.

TIP
Use whatever strength and sweetness of molasses you like best. You can always drizzle some over your muffin halves before eating them, too.

Corny Cornmeal Muffins

Makes 4 large muffins
Prep. Time: 20 minutes ❧ Cooking Time: 2 hours
Ideal slow-cooker size: 6- or 7-quart oval

½ cup flour

½ cup yellow cornmeal

2 ¾ Tbsp. sugar

1 ½ tsp. baking powder

½ tsp. salt

1 Tbsp. finely chopped onion

½ cup cream-style corn

¼ cup mayonnaise

1 ½ Tbsp. vegetable oil

1 small egg

1. In a good-sized bowl, mix together all dry ingredients—flour, cornmeal, sugar, baking powder, and salt.

2. Make a well in the middle of the dry ingredients and add chopped onion, corn, mayo, oil, and egg. Stir just until lightly mixed.

3. Grease interior of four 3-oz. ramekins. Divide batter evenly among the ramekins.

4. Place filled ramekins into slow cooker crock. Cover with slow cooker lid.

5. Bake on High 2 hours, or until tester inserted into center of ramekins comes out clean.

6. Put on oven mitts and lift ramekins out of crock and onto wire baking rack to cool. Or use a sturdy pair of tongs to lift them out.

7. Serve muffins warm or at room temperature.

Why I like this recipe—
A lot of cornbread turns out dry. But this one, because of the creamed corn and mayonnaise, is lusciously moist. The chopped onion adds to its savory flavor.

Savory Cheese Muffins

Makes 4 large muffins
Prep. Time: 20–30 minutes   Cooking Time: 2 hours
Ideal slow-cooker size: 6- or 7-quart oval

1 cup flour

1 Tbsp. baking powder

¼ tsp. salt

4 Tbsp. (½ stick) butter, softened

2 Tbsp. sugar

1 egg

½ cup milk

½ cup grated sharp cheddar cheese

½ tsp. dried basil, *or* 1½ tsp. chopped fresh basil

1. Sift flour, baking powder and salt into a bowl.

2. In a separate, good-sized, bowl, beat together butter and sugar until creamy and light.

3. Add egg and beat well.

4. Add dry ingredients to wet, alternating with milk.

5. Quickly fold in grated cheese and basil, just until blended.

6. Grease interior of four 3-oz. ramekins. Divide batter equally among them.

7. Place ramekins into slow cooker crock. Cover with slow cooker lid.

8. Bake on High 2 hours, or until tester inserted into center of ramekins comes out clean.

9. Wearing oven mitts, lift ramekins out of crock and place on wire baking rack to cool. Or use a pair of sturdy tongs to get them out.

10. Serve muffins warm or at room temperature.

TIP

Savory muffins are sooo good. But you might want to tip off the people eating them so they aren't expecting a bite of sweetness!

Cakes from Scratch

Best Pineapple Cake

Makes 12–16 servings
Prep. Time: 20 minutes ❧ Cooking Time: 2½–3 hours
Ideal slow-cooker size: 5- or 6-quart

2 cups flour

2 cups sugar

2 tsp. baking powder

2 eggs

I tsp. vanilla

20-oz. can crushed pineapple, undrained

I cup chopped nuts

Topping:

3-oz. pkg. cream cheese, softened

4 Tbsp. (½ stick) butter, softened

¾ cup confectioners sugar

¼ tsp. vanilla

¼ cup chopped nuts

1. Mix together flour, sugar, and baking powder in a big bowl.

2. Stir in eggs, vanilla, and undrained pineapple.

3. When well blended, stir in nuts.

4. Grease interior of baking insert or baking dish that fits in your slow cooker.

5. Pour in batter. Cover with lid or greased foil.

6. Place baking insert or dish in slow cooker. Cover with slow cooker lid.

7. Bake on High 2½–3 hours, or until tester inserted in center comes out clean.

8. When cake is full baked, carefully remove insert or dish from cooker. Place on wire baking rack and let cool completely.

9. When cake is nearly cool, mix together cream cheese, butter, sugar, and vanilla. Spread over cooled cake. Sprinkle with chopped nuts.

10. Cut into wedges and serve.

Why I like this recipe—

Whenever I serve this, no one can believe how moist and wonderfully fruity this cake is. I made a batch for my daughter's Supper Club, and she said, "I've never heard guys use the word 'tender' to describe a cake before!"

Cherry Swirl Cake

Makes 12–14 servings
Prep Time: 10–20 minutes ❦ *Cooking Time: 3–4 hours*
Ideal slow-cooker size: 6- or 7-quart oval

¾ cup sugar

4 Tbsp. (half a stick) butter, softened

¼ cup shortening

¾ tsp. baking powder

½ tsp. vanilla

½ tsp. almond extract

2 eggs

1½ cups flour

half a 21-oz. can cherry pie filling

Glaze:

½ cup confectioners sugar

½–1 Tbsp. milk

1. Mix all cake ingredients together except pie filling. Stir just until mixed.

2. Grease a loaf pan. Spread ⅔ of batter into pan.

3. Spread pie filling over batter.

4. Drop remaining batter by tablespoonfuls onto pie filling. Spread batter over pie filling as well as you can, but it's okay if you can't cover it completely. With a knife, swirl the batter through the pie filling—but don't stir or you'll lose the swirl effect.

5. Cover loaf pan with greased foil. Place pan into slow cooker crock. Cover with cooker lid.

6. Bake on High for 3–4 hours, or until tester inserted in center comes out clean.

7. Carefully remove pan from crock. Place on wire baking rack, uncovered, and allow to cool.

8. When cake is just warm, stir glaze ingredients together and then drizzle over cake.

9. Slice and serve.

Why I like this recipe—

This is good for breakfast, good for lunch, good anytime! The bread is absolutely fabulous as a quick bread, sliced and toasted and spread with butter while warm. My daughter declared, "I will eat the whole loaf myself!" And she nearly did.

One-Pot Strawberry Shortcake

Makes 10–12 servings

Prep. Time: 15 minutes ❧ *Cooking Time: 2½–3 hours*

Ideal slow-cooker size: 6-quart oval

2 Tbsp. (¼ stick) butter

1 cup sugar

2 eggs

2½ cups flour

½ tsp. salt

2 tsp. baking powder

1 cup milk

1 tsp. vanilla

1. Melt butter in good-sized, microwave-safe bowl.

2. Stir in sugar and eggs thoroughly.

3. Add flour, salt and baking powder. Mix together until crumbly.

4. Stir in milk and vanilla until well mixed. (The batter won't be completely smooth, but that's okay.)

5. Grease loaf pan.

6. Pour batter into loaf pan. Cover with greased foil.

7. Set in oval slow cooker. Cover cooker.

8. Bake on High for 2½–3 hours, or until tester inserted in center comes out clean.

9. Allow to cool for 20–30 minutes before slicing and serving.

Why I like this recipe—

Don't you love a recipe that you can mix up in only one dish? And one that calls for ingredients you've got on hand? This recipe lets the strawberries shine! In strawberry season, we make this our dinner.

Rhubarb Sour Cream Cake

Makes 10 servings
Prep. Time: 35 minutes   ❧   Cooking Time: 3 hours
Ideal slow-cooker size: 6-quart oval

4 Tbsp. (½ stick) butter, softened

¾ cup brown sugar, firmly packed

1 egg

1 Tbsp. vanilla

2 cups flour

1 tsp. baking soda

1 tsp. salt

1 cup sour cream

2 cups rhubarb, cut into ½"-thick pieces

½ cup sugar

½ tsp. cinnamon

dash of nutmeg

1. In a large bowl, cream butter and brown sugar together until fluffy.

2. Beat in egg and vanilla.

3. In a separate bowl, sift flour with baking soda and salt. Stir into creamed ingredients.

4. Fold in sour cream and rhubarb pieces.

5. Grease full-sized loaf pan.

6. Spoon batter into loaf pan.

7. Mix together ½ cup sugar, ½ tsp. cinnamon, and dash of nutmeg. Sprinkle over batter.

8. Cover loaf pan with foil. Place filled pan in oval slow cooker. Cover with cooker lid.

9. Bake on High 3 hours, or until tester inserted in center of cake comes out clean.

10. Remove pan carefully from slow cooker. Place on wire baking rack to cool 20–30 minutes. Serve warm or at room temperature.

Why I like this recipe—

If you love rhubarb and are always on the prowl for good recipes that include it, add this one to your list. There's something about the balance between sweet and tart here that's irresistible.

Lotsa Blueberries Cake

Makes 8 servings
Prep. Time: 15 minutes ❦ Cooking Time 2–3 hours
Ideal slow-cooker size: 5-quart (or 6- or 7-quart oval)

1 egg
1 cup sugar
3 Tbsp. butter, melted
½ cup milk
2 cups flour
1 tsp. baking powder
pinch of salt
1 pint fresh blueberries

1. Cream together egg, sugar, and butter.

2. Add milk and mix well.

3. Stir in flour, baking powder, and salt. Mix again.

4. Fold blueberries into this stiff batter.

5. Grease interior of loaf pan, slow cooker baking insert, or baking dish that fits in your slow cooker.

6. Cover either with greased foil or lid of baking insert or baking dish.

7. Place baking container into slow cooker crock. Cover with cooker lid.

8. Bake on High 2–3 hours, or until tester inserted in center comes out clean.

9. When finished baking, carefully remove baking container from crock. Set on wire baking rack to cool.

10. When cool, slice and serve.

TIP

You can make this out of blueberry season by using frozen blueberries. Don't thaw them. Just toss the frozen berries with a tablespoon or two of flour in a bowl before stirring them into the batter (in Step 4). Continue with the recipe—and you'll love the outcome!

Banana Nut Cake

Makes 12–14 servings

Prep. Time: 20 minutes ❧ Cooking Time: 2½–3 hours ❧ Ideal slow-cooker size: 5-quart (or 6- or 7-quart oval)

2 cups flour

1 tsp. baking powder

1 tsp. baking soda

½ tsp. salt

1½ cups sugar

½ cup shortening

½ cup buttermilk*

1½ cups sliced bananas

2 eggs

1 tsp. vanilla

½ cup chopped nuts

Banana Frosting:

4 Tbsp. (half a stick) butter, softened

½ tsp. vanilla

1¾ cups, *or a bit more,* confectioners sugar

2 Tbsp. mashed bananas

½ tsp. lemon juice

*If you don't have buttermilk, put 1½ tsp. lemon juice *or* white vinegar in a ½-cup measure. Fill measuring cup with milk. Stir. Let stand 5–7 minutes. Then add to wet ingredients, including any curds that have formed.

1. Sift flour, baking powder, baking soda, and salt together in a good-sized mixing bowl.

2. Combine sugar, shortening, buttermilk, bananas, eggs, and vanilla in a food processor until smooth.

3. Pour wet ingredients into dry. Add nuts. Mix just until combined.

4. Grease and flour a baking insert, baking dish, or loaf pan that fits in your slow cooker.

5. Pour in batter.

6. Cover with lid of insert or dish, or with greased foil. Place container in slow cooker crock. Cover with cooker lid.

7. Bake on High for 2½–3 hours, or until tester inserted in center of cake comes out clean.

8. Carefully remove pan from cooker. Place on wire baking rack, uncovered, and allow to cool.

9. While cake is cooling, make frosting. Cream together butter and vanilla by hand or with an electric mixer until well mixed. Gradually beat in sugar. Stir in bananas and lemon juice. Spread over cooled cake.

TIP

You've got bananas two ways here—sliced and smashed. You'll be all right if you've got three medium-sized ones. Don't skip the frosting—just mix it up with no cooking required.

Pumpkin Cake

Makes 12 servings

Prep. Time: 20 minutes ❧ *Cooking Time: 2½–3 hours* ❧ *Ideal slow-cooker size: 5- or 6-quart*

2 eggs

1 cup sugar

¾ cup vegetable oil

1½ cups flour

1½ tsp. baking powder

1 tsp. cinnamon

1 tsp. baking soda

pinch of salt

¼ tsp. ground ginger

1 cup pumpkin

½ cup chopped walnuts

Cream Cheese Frosting:

4 Tbsp. (half a stick) butter, softened

3-oz. pkg. Philadelphia cream cheese, softened

2 cups confectioners sugar

1 tsp. vanilla

1. Beat the eggs well in a large bowl. Stir in the sugar and blend well.

2. Beat in the oil.

3. In a separate bowl, stir together flour, baking powder, cinnamon, baking soda, salt, and ground ginger.

4. Add the dry ingredients alternately with the pumpkin to the wet.

5. When well mixed, stir in the walnuts.

6. Grease and flour a baking insert or baking dish that fits into your slow cooker.

7. Spoon batter into insert or dish. Cover with its lid or greased foil.

8. Place filled insert or dish into cooker. Cover with the cooker lid.

9. Bake on High 2½–3 hours, or until tester inserted in center comes out clean.

10. Carefully remove insert or dish from cooker and place on wire baking rack.

11. Allow to cool, uncovered.

12. Meanwhile, make the cream cheese frosting. Stir butter and cream cheese together until smooth.

13. Carefully fold in sugar. Stir in vanilla.

14. When cake is completely cooled, cover with frosting.

15. Cut in half, and then in wedges to serve.

Peachy Gingerbread

Makes 12–14 servings

Prep. Time: 20–30 minutes ❦ Cooking Time: 2½–3 ½ hours

Ideal slow-cooker size: 6- or 7-quart oval

⅓ cup butter, softened

½ cup brown sugar

½ cup strong molasses

I egg

1¾ cups flour

½ tsp. salt

I tsp. baking powder

½ tsp. baking soda

1½ tsp. ground ginger

I tsp. cinnamon

¾ cup sour milk *or* buttermilk*

2 cups canned sliced peaches, well drained

*If you don't have sour milk *or* buttermilk, place I Tbsp. in a I cup-measure. Pour in milk to the ¾-cup line. Stir. Let stand for 5–10 minutes. Then add to batter according to instructions below, including the curds if some have formed.

1. Cream butter and sugar together, beating until fluffy.

2. Add molasses and egg and beat until well mixed.

3. In a separate bowl, stir together flour, salt, baking powder, baking soda, ginger, and cinnamon.

4. Add dry ingredients to wet ingredients, alternately with sour milk. Beat well after each addition.

5. Grease interior of loaf pan. Cover bottom with well-drained sliced peaches.

6. Pour batter over peaches. Cover with greased foil.

7. Place pan into slow cooker crock. Cover with crock lid.

8. Bake on High for 2½–3 ½ hours, or until tester inserted in center of cake comes out clean.

9. Carefully remove pan from crock. Place on wire baking rack. Allow to cool. Serve warm or at room temperature, making sure to scoop out peaches from the bottom with each serving.

TIP

I like to use B'rer Rabbit Molasses's green label (mild flavor) for this recipe so the strength of the molasses doesn't overwhelm the peach flavor.

Gingerbread with Lemon Sauce

Makes 10 servings ❦ *Prep. Time: 20–30 minutes* ❦ *Cooking Time: 2–3 hours*
Ideal slow-cooker size: 5-quart (or 6- or 7-quart oval)

2 cups flour

I cup sugar

I tsp. ground ginger

I tsp. ground cinnamon

½ cup shortening

I egg, beaten

2 Tbsp. strong molasses

½ tsp. salt

I tsp. baking soda

I cup buttermilk*

whipped cream, *optional*

Lemon Sauce:

2 cups water

4 Tbsp. cornstarch

1½ cups sugar

¼ tsp. salt

3 egg yolks

1½ Tbsp. butter

juice of 2 lemons

zest of I lemon

*If you don't have buttermilk, put I Tbsp. lemon juice *or* white vinegar in a I-cup measure. Fill the cup with milk. Stir. Let stand for 5–10 minutes. Then pour into batter according to instructions, curds and all.

1. To make the gingerbread, sift flour, sugar, ginger, and cinnamon into large bowl. Mix together.

2. Cut shortening into flour mixture to make fine crumbs.

3. Take out ½ cup crumbs and set aside.

4. To crumbs remaining in mixing bowl, add egg, molasses, salt, baking soda, and buttermilk (or your substitute). Beat well.

5. Grease and flour either a baking insert, a baking dish or a loaf pan that fits into your slow cooker.

6. Pour batter into baking container. Sprinkle with ½ cup reserved crumbs.

7. Place baking container into slow cooker crock. Cover with the container's lid or greased foil. Cover slow cooker with its lid.

8. Bake on High 2–3 hours, or until tester inserted in center of gingerbread comes out clean.

9. Carefully remove container from cooker. Place on wire baking rack and uncover to cool.

10. To make lemon sauce while gingerbread is baking, bring water to boil in saucepan.

11. Combine cornstarch, sugar, and salt in a bowl, mixing well.

12. Whisk dry ingredients into boiling water, stirring constantly. Cook about 5 minutes over low heat until mixture thickens.

Why I like this recipe—

This sturdy, old-fashioned dessert gets a nice lift from the lemon sauce made with fresh lemons. The sauce isn't required, of course, but it adds a good zing.

13. Beat egg yolks in a bowl. Stir a small amount of hot sugar mixture into beaten yolks, whisking continually.

14. Return the whole mixture to the pan and cook 1 more minute, stirring constantly.

15. Remove from heat. Add butter, lemon juice, and lemon zest. Stir to combine.

16. Serve over warm slices of gingerbread. Top with whipped cream, if you wish.

Shoofly Cake

Makes 8–10 servings
Prep. Time: 20–30 minutes   ☙   Cooking Time: 2½–3 hours
Ideal slow-cooker size: 6- or 7-quart oval

2 cups flour

1 cup + 2 Tbsp. brown sugar

8 Tbsp. (1 stick) butter, softened

½ cup light molasses*

1 cup boiling water

1 tsp. baking soda

*In eastern Pennsylvania, where Shoofly has its roots, King Syrup is preferred over light molasses. Use it if you can find it.

1. Combine flour, sugar, and butter in a good-sized bowl. Work into fine crumbs with your fingers.

2. Scoop out 1½ cups crumbs and reserve for topping the cake.

3. Add molasses, boiling water, and baking soda to crumbs left in the bowl. Mix together well.

4. Grease and flour a loaf pan. Pour thin batter into pan. Sprinkle with reserved 1½ cups crumbs.

5. Cover pan with greased foil, and then place in oval cooker. Cover with cooker lid.

6. Bake on High for 2½–3 hours, or until tester inserted in center comes out clean.

7. Carefully remove pan from slow cooker. Place on wire baking rack to cool.

8. Serve warm or at room temperature, as is, or topped with ice cream. (Some people like it in a cereal bowl with milk—for breakfast!)

Why I like this recipe—

So the story goes that cooks in eastern Pennsylvania in 19th century America cooled their cakes and pies on the windowsill. And the sweetness of this sturdy cake drew flies. Today it draws oohs and aahs, especially when it's served warm.

Spice Cake

Makes 12 servings
Prep. Time: 20 minutes   ❦   Cooking Time: 2–3 hours
Ideal slow-cooker size: 6- or 7-quart oval

2 cups brown sugar

8 Tbsp. (1 stick) butter, softened

2 eggs

1 cup sour milk*

2½ cups sifted flour

1½ tsp. baking powder

1 tsp. cinnamon

1 tsp. nutmeg

1 tsp. baking soda

1 tsp. vanilla

Caramel Icing:

4 Tbsp. (½ stick) butter

½ cup brown sugar

2 Tbsp. milk

¾–1 cup confectioners sugar

*To make sour milk, put 1 Tbsp. lemon juice *or* white vinegar in a 1-cup measure. Then fill the cup with milk. Stir. Let stand for 5–10 minutes. It will curdle slightly, as it's supposed to do. Use the whole works in the batter.

1. Cream sugar and butter together until fluffy.

2. Add eggs and beat until mixture is light.

3. In a separate bowl, sift together flour, baking powder, cinnamon, nutmeg, and baking soda. Mix together well.

4. Add dry ingredients alternately with the sour milk to the creamed ingredients. Beat well after each addition.

5. Stir in vanilla.

6. Grease and flour a loaf pan. Pour batter into pan. Cover with greased foil.

7. Place loaf pan into slow cooker crock. Cover with slow cooker lid.

8. Bake on High 2–3 hours, or until tester inserted in center comes out clean.

9. When finished baking, carefully remove pan from cooker. Set on wire baking rack to cool.

10. When cake is nearly cooled to room temperature, make icing. Melt butter in saucepan. Stir in brown sugar, stirring continually over heat for two minutes. Add milk. Continue stirring until mixture comes to a boil. Remove from heat and let cool. Sift ¾ cup confectioners sugar over caramel mixture. Stir in until smooth. Sift in more if needed until icing can be spread over the cooled cake.

11. When cake is completely cooled, spread with caramel icing.

Why I like this recipe—

I don't remember when or how I fell in love with Spice Cake since I can never get enough chocolate. But it was always the cake I told Grandma I would like when she asked what kind I wanted for my birthday. I am thinking now that it might have something to do with the caramel icing that she always piled onto it. Anyway, it is an old-fashioned cake, but still great for any age. And it bakes up perfectly in a slow cooker!

Chocolate Applesauce Cake

Makes 12–15 servings
Prep. Time: 20 minutes ❦ *Cooking Time: 2½–3 hours*
Ideal slow-cooker size: 5- or 6-quart

1½ cups sugar

½ cup oil

2 eggs

2 cups applesauce

2 cups flour

1½ tsp. baking soda

½ tsp. cinnamon

2 Tbsp. unsweetened
cocoa powder

Topping:

3 Tbsp. sugar

1 cup chocolate chips

½ cup chopped nuts, *optional*

1. In a medium-sized bowl, combine 1½ cups sugar, oil, eggs, and applesauce, mixing well.

2. Add flour, baking soda, cinnamon, and cocoa powder. Stir together thoroughly.

3. Grease and flour a baking insert or baking dish that fits in your slow cooker.

4. Pour batter into insert or baking dish.

5. In a small bowl, mix sugar and chocolate chips together, plus chopped nuts if you wish.

6. Sprinkle over batter.

7. Cover with insert or baking dish lid, or foil. Place in slow cooker crock. Cover with cooker lid.

8. Bake on High 2½–3 hours, or until tester inserted in center of cake comes out clean.

9. Carefully remove insert or baking dish from cooker. Place on wire baking rack and uncover. Allow to cool for 20–30 minutes before slicing to serve.

Why I like this recipe—

You get away with fewer calories in this cake because of the 2 cups of applesauce. But you don't suffer when you eat it. The chocolate chips—and pick your favorite variety of chocolate—melt beguilingly into the cake.

Deep and Dark Chocolate Cake

Makes 12 servings

Prep. Time: 20 minutes ❧ Cooking Time: 3½ hours

Ideal slow-cooker size: 5- or 6-quart

1 tsp. baking powder

2 tsp. baking soda

2 cups flour

pinch of salt, *optional*

2 cups sugar

¾ cup unsweetened cocoa powder

2 eggs

½ cup vegetable oil

1 cup hot strong coffee

1 cup milk

2 tsp. vanilla

Icing:

2 cups confectioners sugar

1 Tbsp. butter, melted

1 cup peanut butter, smooth *or* chunky

1 tsp. vanilla

milk, enough to spread icing

1. In a large bowl, combine baking powder, baking soda, flour, and salt if you wish.

2. Stir in sugar and cocoa powder.

3. Beat in eggs. Add oil, coffee, milk, and vanilla. Mix together well. Batter will be thin and runny.

4. Grease and flour interior of baking insert or baking dish that fits in your slow cooker. Pour batter into insert or dish.

5. Cover with lid of insert or dish, or foil. Place in slow cooker crock. Cover slow cooker.

6. Cook on High 2–3 hours, or until tester inserted in middle of cake comes out clean.

7. When the cake is done, carefully lift the insert or dish out of the crock, set it on a wire rack, and let it cool for 20–30 minutes before cutting and serving.

8. If you wish, and after the cake has cooled, ice it with Peanut Butter Icing: Cream together sugar, butter, and peanut butter.

9. Add vanilla and enough milk (begin with 1–2 Tbsp.) to make icing spread easily.

TIP

I have a 2½-qt. baking insert that fits perfectly inside my 5-qt. slow cooker. When I bake this cake in it, it stands taller than a single layer cake, and I don't need to worry about balancing layers so they're straight and even. This is among my most favorite cakes!

Light and Fluffy Chocolate Chip Cheesecake

Makes 30 1" square servings

Prep. Time: 20–30 minutes ❦ Cooking Time: 1½–2 hours ❦ Chilling Time: 3 hours
Ideal slow-cooker size: 6-quart oval

3 eggs

¾ cup sugar

3 8-oz. pkgs. cream cheese, softened

1 tsp. vanilla

1½ 16-oz. rolls refrigerated* chocolate chip cookie dough**

whipped cream, *optional*

chocolate topping, *optional*

*Keep the dough refrigerated until you're ready to use it. It's easiest to work with when it's stiff.

**You'll have half a roll left over to make cookies.

1. Place all ingredients except cookie dough in large mixer or food processor bowl.

2. Blend together just until creamy, about 20–30 seconds. Do not overmix. Set aside.

3. Slice cookie dough into ¼"-thick slices. Set aside 9 slices.

4. Lightly grease interior of slow cooker crock. Lay remaining slices over bottom of cooker. Pat them together to form a solid crust.

5. Spoon in cream cheese mixture. Spread over cookie crust.

6. Arrange the reserved 9 cookie slices on top of cream-cheese mixture.

7. Cover cooker. Bake on High for 1½–2 hours, or until cookies are baked but not burned and cream cheese sets up.

8. Uncover and allow to cool to room temperature.

9. Then refrigerate for 3 hours or more. When firm, cut into 1" squares.

10. If you wish, top with whipped cream and/or chocolate topping to serve.

TIP

Have your nose on alert while you're baking this cheesecake. If your slow cooker cooks hot, flip it off the minute you smell that the cookie crust might be getting dark. Leave the cheesecake in the crock for another hour so that the creamy filling sets up, without the crust burning.

Shortcut Cakes

Summer Breezes Cake

Makes 10–12 servings
Prep. Time: 20 minutes ❦ *Cooking Time: 2½–3½ hours*
Ideal slow-cooker size: 5-quart

18¼-oz. box yellow cake mix

11-oz. can mandarin oranges, undrained

4 eggs

½ cup cooking oil

Frosting:

½ cup whipped topping, thawed

8-oz. can crushed pineapple, drained

3-oz. pkg. instant vanilla pudding

1. Grease and flour interior of slow cooker crock.

2. In a large mixing bowl, thoroughly combine dry cake mix, undrained oranges, eggs, and cooking oil.

3. Pour into prepared crock, spreading batter out evenly.

4. Cover. Bake on High 2½–3½ hours, or until tester inserted into center of cake comes out clean.

5. Uncover, making sure that condensation on inside of cooker lid doesn't drip on finished cake.

6. Remove crock from cooker and allow cake to cool completely.

7. When cake is cooled, prepare frosting by folding together whipped topping, drained crushed pineapple, and dry pudding mix.

8. Spread over cake. Refrigerate until ready to serve cake, sliced, or spooned out of crock.

Why I like this recipe—
So fruity. So light. So easy and delicious.

Blueberry Swirl Cake

Makes 10–12 servings
Prep. Time: 15–20 minutes ❦ *Cooking Time: 3 ½–4 hours*
Ideal slow-cooker size: 5-quart

3-oz. pkg. cream cheese, softened
18¼-oz. box white cake mix
3 eggs
3 Tbsp. water
21-oz. can blueberry pie filling

1. Grease and flour interior of slow cooker crock.

2. Beat cream cheese in a large mixing bowl until soft and creamy.

3. Stir in dry cake mix, eggs, and water. Blend well with cream cheese.

4. Pour batter into prepared crock, spreading it out evenly.

5. Pour blueberry pie filling over top of batter.

6. Swirl blueberries and batter by zigzagging a table knife through the batter.

7. Cover. Bake on High 3½–4 hours, or until a tester inserted into center of cake comes out clean.

8. Uncover, being careful to not let condensation from lid drop on finished cake.

9. Remove crock from cooker.

10. Serve cake warm or at room temperature.

Why I like this recipe—

Keep a box of the cake mix and a can of blueberry pie filling in your pantry, and a package of cream cheese in the fridge, and you're set up for spontaneous guests. Invite everyone back for dessert after a soccer game or a movie—and serve them this. Remember, it's been cooking while you've been out having fun!

Lightly White Pear Cake

Makes 10–12 servings
Prep. Time: 15–20 minutes ❧ Cooking Time: 3 ½–4 hours
Ideal slow-cooker size: 5-quart

15¼-oz. can pears (you're going to chop them, so buy pear pieces if you can find them)

18¼-oz. pkg. white cake mix

1 egg

2 egg whites

2 tsp. confectioners sugar

1. Grease and flour interior of slow cooker crock.

2. Fish pears out of syrup to chop them, but keep the syrup.

3. Place chopped pears and syrup into electric mixing bowl. Add dry cake mix, egg and egg whites.

4. Beat with electric mixer on low speed for 30 seconds, and then on high speed for 4 minutes.

5. Spoon batter into prepared crock, spreading it out evenly.

6. Cover cooker. Bake on High 3½–4 hours, or until tester inserted in center of cake comes out clean.

7. Uncover without letting condensation drip on cake. Remove crock from cooker. Allow to cool completely.

8. Dust with confectioners sugar before slicing or spooning out to serve.

Why I like this recipe—
Light and lovely! And
subtly flavored.

Sour Cream Peach Cake

Makes 10–12 servings
Prep. Time: 15 minutes ❧ *Cooking Time: 3½–4 hours*
Ideal slow-cooker size: 5-quart

18¼-oz. box orange-flavored cake mix

21-oz. can peach pie filling

½ cup sour cream

2 eggs

confectioners sugar *or* whipped topping

1. Grease and flour interior of slow cooker crock.

2. Mix dry cake mix, pie filling, sour cream, and eggs together until thoroughly blended.

3. Pour batter into prepared crock, spreading it out evenly.

4. Cover. Bake on High 3½–4 hours, or until tester inserted into center of cake comes out clean.

5. Remove crock from cooker and allow to cool to room temperature.

6. Sprinkle cake with confectioners sugar, or spread with whipped topping just before serving.

Why I like this recipe—

Our one daughter's birthday is in late July, and she loves peach desserts. So I'm always on the hunt for good peach dishes. Here's a downright delicious one that you can eat at any time of the year because it doesn't depend on fresh peaches.

Sunny Spice Cake

Makes 10–12 servings
Prep. Time: 15 minutes 🎔 Cooking Time: 2½–3 ½ hours
Ideal slow-cooker size: 5-quart

18¼-oz. box spice cake mix

3⅝-oz. pkg. butterscotch instant pudding

2 cups milk

2 eggs

10–12 fresh *or* canned peach halves, drained if canned

9-oz. container frozen whipped topping, thawed

1. Grease and flour interior of slow cooker crock.

2. In a mixing bowl, blend together cake mix, pudding mix, milk, and eggs.

3. Pour into prepared crock, spreading batter out evenly.

4. Cover. Bake on High 2½–3½ hours, or until tester inserted into center of cake comes out clean.

5. Uncover, being careful not to let condensation from inside of lid drip on finished cake.

6. Remove crock from cooker and let cool.

7. When ready to serve, cut into serving-size pieces. Place a peach half on each serving of cake. Top each with a dollop of whipped topping.

Why I like this recipe—

A combination you might not have thought of putting together, but the peaches are a wonderful addition, plus you don't need to make frosting.

Spicy Chocolate Pumpkin Cake

Makes 10–12 servings
Prep. Time: 15–20 minutes   ❦   Cooking Time: 3½–4 hours
Ideal slow-cooker size: 5-quart

18¼-oz. box spice cake mix

½ cup water

½ cup vegetable oil

3 large eggs

half an 8-oz. pkg. cream cheese, softened

1 cup canned *or* cooked pumpkin

6 squares semisweet baking chocolate, coarsely chopped

1. Grease and flour interior of slow cooker crock.

2. Using an electric mixer, blend together cake mix, water, oil, and eggs.

3. Blend in cream cheese and pumpkin, beating on medium speed.

4. Stir in chopped chocolate.

5. Pour into prepared crock, smoothing it out evenly.

6. Cover. Bake on High 3½–4 hours, or until tester inserted into center of cake comes out clean.

7. Uncover, making sure condensation on inside of lid doesn't drip on finished cake.

8. Remove crock from cooker and allow cake to cool.

9. When cake is completely cool, frost with cream cheese frosting (recipe on page xx) if you wish.

TIP

Wowser. Talk about flavor. This brings two of my great flavor loves together— chocolate and spice cakes. Go another step and top it with cream cheese frosting (see recipe on p. 103) if you dare.

Unbelievable Carrot Cake

Makes 12–14 servings
Prep. Time: 15 minutes ❧ *Cooking Time: 3½–4 hours*
Ideal slow-cooker size: 6- or 7-quart oval

2-layer spice cake mix

2 cups (½ lb.) shredded carrots

1 cup crushed pineapple
with juice

3 egg whites

½ cup All-Bran cereal

Cream Cheese Frosting:

3-oz. pkg. cream cheese, softened

¼ cup (half a stick) butter,
softened

2 cups confectioners sugar

1 tsp. vanilla

milk (start with 1 Tbsp. and
increase gradually
if you need more)

1. Combine the dry cake mix, shredded carrots, crushed pineapple with juice, egg whites, and All-Bran cereal thoroughly in a big bowl.

2. Grease and flour a loaf pan.

3. Pour batter into prepared pan.

4. Cover with greased foil and place in slow cooker.

5. Cover cooker with its lid.

6. Bake on High for 3½–4 hours, or until tester inserted in center of cake comes out clean.

7. Carefully remove pan from cooker. Place on wire baking rack to cool, uncovered.

8. As the cake cools, make the frosting by mixing together the softened cream cheese and butter, confectioners sugar and vanilla. When well combined, stir in milk, starting with 1 Tbsp. and adding more if necessary, until the frosting becomes spreadable.

9. Frost cake when it's completely cooled.

10. Slice and serve.

TIP

No need to shred carrots yourself anymore if you're short on time. You can buy them shredded.

Moist and Creamy Coconut Cake

Makes 10–12 servings

Prep. Time: 20 minutes ❧ *Cooking Time: 2½–3½ hours* ❧ *Chilling Time: 8 hours or overnight*
Ideal slow-cooker size: 5-quart

18¼-oz. box yellow cake mix

1¼ cups milk

½ cup sugar

2 cups flaked unsweetened coconut, *divided*

9-oz. container frozen whipped topping, thawed

1 tsp. vanilla

1. Grease and flour interior of slow cooker crock.

2. Prepare cake mix as directed on package.

3. Spoon into prepared crock, smoothing batter out evenly.

4. Bake on High 2½–3½ hours, or until tester inserted into center of cake comes out clean.

5. Uncover, making sure that condensation on inside of lid doesn't drip onto finished cake.

6. Remove crock from cooker and allow to cool for 15 minutes.

7. Meanwhile, combine milk, sugar, and ½ cup coconut in a saucepan. Bring to a boil, stirring frequently. Reduce heat and simmer 1 minute.

8. Spoon evenly over warm cake. Let cool completely.

9. Fold together ½ cup coconut, whipped topping, and vanilla. Spread over cooled cake.

10. Sprinkle remaining coconut evenly over top of cake.

11. Cover and chill overnight in fridge.

12. Slice, or spoon out of crock, to serve.

TIP

You've got three toppings going here—which is what makes this cake such a stand-out, especially for coconut lovers. Make sure you've got enough time to chill the finished cake for 8 hours before serving it.

Apple German Chocolate Cake

Makes 10–12 servings
Prep. Time: 15–20 minutes ❦ Cooking Time: 3½–4 hours
Ideal slow-cooker size: 5-quart

21-oz. can apple pie filling

18¼-oz. box German chocolate cake mix

3 eggs

¾ cup coarsely chopped walnuts

½ cup miniature semisweet chocolate chips

1. Grease and flour interior of slow cooker crock.

2. Place pie filling in blender or food processor. Cover and process until apples are in ¼" chunks.

3. If using food processor, add dry cake mix and eggs. Process until smooth. (If you used a blender for the apples, pour them into an electric mixer bowl, add dry cake mix and eggs, and beat on medium speed for 5 minutes.)

4. Pour into prepared slow cooker crock.

5. Sprinkle with walnuts and chocolate chips.

6. Cover. Bake on High 3½–4 hours, or until tester inserted into center of cake comes out clean.

7. Remove crock from cooker. Allow to cool completely before serving.

Why I like this recipe—

Chocolate goes with everything, right? The apples here add a comforting tenderness, but they let the chocolate reign.

Quick Chocolate Fudge Cake

Makes 10–12 servings

Prep. Time: 15 minutes ❧ *Cooking Time: 2½–3½ hours*

Ideal slow-cooker size: 5-quart

18¼-oz. box chocolate fudge cake mix, or German chocolate cake mix

2 eggs

21-oz. can cherry pie filling

1 tsp. vanilla *or* almond extract, *optional*

1. Grease and flour interior of slow cooker crock.

2. In a good-sized bowl, mix together dry cake mix, eggs, pie filling, and extract if you wish. Batter will be pretty stiff.

3. Spoon into greased and floured crock.

4. Cover with slow cooker lid.

5. Bake on High 2½–3½ hours, or until tester inserted into center of cake comes out clean.

6. Remove crock from cooker and allow to cool, uncovered.

7. Serve from crock, either in wedges, or spoonfuls.

TIP

Drops of water will gather on the inside of the slow cooker lid while the cake bakes. To keep the water from dripping onto the finished cake, remove the lid by lifting it quickly and swooping it away from yourself.

Bars
and
Brownies

Chocolate Pecan Pie Bars

Makes 24 servings
Prep. Time: 20–30 minutes ❧ Cooking Time: 2½–3 hours
Ideal slow-cooker size: 6-quart oval

8 Tbsp. (1 stick) butter, softened

¼ cup brown sugar, packed

1¼ cups flour

½ tsp. salt

3 large eggs

¾ cup light corn syrup

½ cup sugar

2 Tbsp. (¼ stick) melted butter

12-oz. pkg., *or* 2 cups, semisweet chocolate chips

2 cups coarsely chopped pecans

TIP

Remember that the crock is hot when you spread the filling over the crust. Don't let your arms get against it.

1. Grease interior of slow cooker crock really well.

2. Cream together 8 Tbsp. butter and brown sugar.

3. Stir in flour and salt until mixture is crumbly.

4. Press mixture into bottom of crock to form crust.

5. Cover. Bake on High 1 hour.

6. Meanwhile, mix eggs, corn syrup, sugar, and 2 Tbsp. melted butter until well blended.

7. Stir in chocolate chips and chopped pecans.

8. When crust is finished baking, uncover. Spread creamy chocolate chip-pecan mixture over crust, being careful not to burn your arms on the hot crock.

9. Cover cooker. Continue baking on High for 1½–2 hours, or until filling is firm in the center.

10. Uncover. Remove crock from cooker. Place on wire baking rack and allow to cool.

11. When bars have reached room temperature, cut into 20 squares and 4 triangles in corners.

Why I like this recipe—

I'm a sucker for chocolate and pecans. This is a combination I can't improve on. I like it best with deep, dark, black coffee.

Turtle Bars

Makes 24 servings
Prep. Time: 20–30 minutes ❧ Cooking Time 3–3½ hours
Ideal slow-cooker size: 6-quart oval

2 cups flour

1¾ cups light brown
sugar, *divided*

20 Tbsp. (2½ sticks) butter,
softened and *divided*

1¼ cups pecan halves

1 cup chocolate chips

1. Grease interior of slow cooker crock.

2. Mix together flour, 1 cup brown sugar, and 8 Tbsp. (1 stick) butter, softened, until crumbly. Pat firmly into bottom of crock.

3. Place pecan halves evenly over crust.

4. Heat remaining ¾ cup brown sugar and remaining 12 Tbsp. (1½ sticks) butter in a saucepan. Boil 1 minute, stirring constantly.

5. Pour over pecan crust.

6. Cover cooker. Bake on High 3–3½ hours, or until mixture is firm.

7. Sprinkle chocolate chips over hot bars. Let stand 2 minutes.

8. Using a knife, swirl chips as they melt, covering the bars as well as you can, but leaving some of the chips whole.

9. Remove crock from cooker and place on a wire baking rack to cool.

10. When room temperature, cut bars into 20 squares and 4 triangles in the corners.

Why I like this recipe—
These are sweet, folks—
just like they're supposed
to be!

Chocolate Chip Pizza

Makes 24 servings
Prep. Time: 25–30 minutes   Cooking Time: 2–2½ hours
Ideal slow-cooker size: 6-quart oval

I cup flour

½ tsp. baking powder

⅛ tsp. baking soda

½ tsp. salt

⅓ cup butter, melted

I cup brown sugar, packed

I egg

I Tbsp. hot water

1¼ tsp. vanilla

½ cup chopped nuts, your choice

I cup chopped M&Ms

I cup mini marshmallows

1. In a medium-sized bowl, sift together flour, baking powder, baking soda, and salt. Set aside.

2. In a good-sized bowl, cream together butter and brown sugar until well blended. Add egg, hot water, and vanilla, mixing well.

3. Add dry ingredients to wet, ⅓ at a time, mixing well after each addition.

4. Stir in chopped nuts.

5. Grease interior of slow cooker crock. Spread batter into crock.

6. Sprinkle with chopped M&Ms and mini marshmallows.

7. Cover. Bake on High 2–2½ hours, or until tester inserted in center comes out clean.

8. Uncover, and place crock on baking rack to cool.

9. When room temperature, cut into 20 squares with 4 triangles in the corners.

TIP

To make it seem more like pizza, cut the finished pizza in half the long way. Then cut wedges, zigzag-fashion from the center cut to the outer edge of the crock.

Cocoa Brownies with Dark Chocolate Frosting

Makes 12 servings
Prep. Time: 20 minutes ❧ Cooking Time: 1½–2 hours
Ideal slow-cooker size: 5- or 5½-quart

1 cup sugar

8 Tbsp. (1 stick) butter, softened

2 eggs

¼ tsp. salt

1 tsp. vanilla

¼ cup unsweetened cocoa powder

¾ cup flour

½ cup chopped nuts, your favorite

Frosting:

1½ cups confectioners sugar

¼ cup unsweetened cocoa powder

4 Tbsp. butter (half a stick), softened

3 Tbsp. cream *or* milk

½ tsp. vanilla

12 pecan halves

1. To make batter, cream sugar and butter together.

2. Add eggs, salt, vanilla, and cocoa powder.

3. Stir in flour and nuts, blending well.

4. Grease interior of slow cooker crock. Spoon batter into crock.

5. Cover. Bake on High 1½–2 hours, or until tester inserted into center comes out clean.

6. Uncover crock and place it on a baking rack to cool.

7. While brownies are cooling, make frosting. Mix confectioners sugar and cocoa powder together.

8. In a good-sized bowl, cream butter until shiny.

9. Add sugar-cocoa mixture to butter alternately with cream or milk.

10. Stir in vanilla until everything is well mixed. (If you want shiny frosting, heat mixture over very low heat for about 5 minutes, stirring continually. Cool for a minute or two, and then spread over brownies.)

11. Cut into 12 brownies. Top each with a pecan half.

TIP

Get the darkest unsweetened cocoa powder you can find. Then these brownies really show off. Cut them small so you can have two!

Double Chocolate Crunch Bars

Makes 24 servings

Prep. Time: 25 minutes ❧ *Cooking Time: 2½–3¼ hours*

Ideal slow-cooker size: 6-quart oval

8 Tbsp. (1 stick) butter

¾ cup sugar

2 eggs

1 tsp. vanilla

¾ cup flour

2 Tbsp. unsweetened cocoa powder

¼ tsp. baking powder

¼ tsp. salt

2 cups mini marshmallows

1 cup chocolate chips

1 cup peanut butter, smooth *or* crunchy

1½ cups crispy rice cereal

1. Melt butter. Stir in sugar and blend well.

2. Beat in eggs and vanilla.

3. Add flour, cocoa powder, baking powder, and salt. Mix well.

4. Grease interior of slow cooker crock. Spread batter evenly over the bottom of the crock.

5. Cover. Bake on High 2½–3¼ hours, or until a tester inserted in center of bar comes out clean.

6. Sprinkle mini marshmallows over bars. Cover and bake for 15 minutes more.

7. Turn cooker off and remove crock. Set on a wire baking rack to cool, uncovered.

8. When bars are nearly at room temperature, place chocolate chips and peanut butter in a microwave-safe bowl. Melt on High for 1 minute. Stir. Microwave for 30 seconds more if not completely melted. Stir. Microwave again if needed.

9. Stir cereal into melted chocolate and peanut butter.

10. Spread cereal mixture over bars.

11. Refrigerate for 3–4 hours.

12. Cut into 20 bars (and 4 triangles on the corners) with a silicon or sturdy plastic knife. Your bars will have firm edges, and you'll have preserved the interior of your crock.

TIP

The mini marshmallows may take a little longer than 15 minutes to melt and become spreadable. I like mine melty, and if you do, too, you might want to switch the cooker to Low, so the brownies don't dry out, and give the marshmallows up to 30 minutes.

Philly Chippers

Makes 24 servings
Prep. Time: 15–20 minutes ❦ *Cooking Time: 2–2½ hours*
Ideal slow-cooker size: 6-quart oval

16 Tbsp. (2 sticks) butter, softened

8-oz. pkg. cream cheese, softened

¾ cup sugar

¾ cup brown sugar

1 egg

1 tsp. vanilla

¼ cup milk

2½ cups flour

1 tsp. baking powder

1 tsp. salt

12-oz. pkg., *or* 2 cups, chocolate chips

1. Grease interior of slow cooker crock.

2. In a large mixing bowl, cream together butter, cream cheese, and sugars.

3. Add egg, vanilla, and milk. Mix well.

4. In a separate bowl, combine flour, baking powder, and salt. Blend dry ingredients into wet.

5. Fold chocolate chips into batter.

6. Pour into crock.

7. Cover. Bake on High 2½–3 hours, or until tester inserted in center of chippers comes out clean.

8. Uncover. Remove crock from cooker. Place on wire baking rack to cool.

9. When chippers reach room temperature, cut into 20 squares and 4 triangles in the corners.

Why I like this recipe—
Think of this as a big chocolate chip cookie. . . . It's every bit as delicious!

Magic Cookie Bars

Makes 24 servings
Prep. Time: 20 minutes ❦ Cooking Time: 2–3 hours
Ideal slow-cooker size: 6-quart oval

8 Tbsp. (1 stick) butter, melted

1½ cups graham cracker crumbs

14-oz. can sweetened condensed milk

6-oz. pkg. semisweet chocolate chips

1 cup peanut butter chips

1 cup shredded coconut, sweetened *or* not

1 cup chopped nuts, your choice

1. Grease interior of slow cooker crock.

2. Pour melted butter into crock.

3. Sprinkle graham cracker crumbs over butter.

4. Gently pour condensed milk over top, being careful not to disturb the crumbs.

5. In a bowl, mix together chocolate and peanut butter chips, coconut, and nuts. Sprinkle evenly over mixture in crock.

6. Cover. Bake on High 2–3 hours, or until firm.

7. Uncover. Lift crock onto wire baking rack and let cool.

8. When room temperature, cut with a silicone or plastic knife into 20 squares and 4 triangles in the corners.

Why I like this recipe—

A new twist on the beloved bars made with stacked ingredients. These never get old.

Gooey Oatmeal Jumble Bars

Makes 24 servings
Prep. Time: 20 minutes ❧ *Cooking Time: 2 hours*
Ideal slow-cooker size: 6-quart oval

3 cups dry oatmeal,
quick *or* old-fashioned

1½ cups flour

1 cup brown sugar

16 Tbsp. (2 sticks)
butter, melted

¾ tsp. salt

½ tsp. baking soda

10–12-oz. jar preserves,
your choice of flavors

1. Grease interior of slow cooker crock.

2. Combine all ingredients, except preserves, in a big bowl, mixing well.

3. Scoop out 1 cup mixture and reserve.

4. Press remaining mixture into bottom of crock.

5. Spread preserves over crumb crust to within ½" of sides of crock (to prevent burning).

6. Sprinkle everything with reserved crumbs.

7. Cover. Bake on High for 2 hours, or until crust is firm.

8. Uncover and remove crock from cooker. Place on wire baking rack to cool.

9. When room temperature, cut bars into 20 squares and 4 triangles in corners.

A great variation—

Ask the kids in your life what kind of preserves to use. Once they've made their choice, they'll be on board for mixing up the other ingredients. Just give them a big enough bowl so they can really wade in.

Crunchy Granola Bars

Makes 24 servings
Prep. Time: 20–30 minutes   ❦   Cooking Time: 2–3 hours
Ideal slow-cooker size: 6-quart oval

2 cups shredded coconut, sweetened *or* not

1½ cups old-fashioned dry oats

1½ cups raisins *or* Craisins®

2 cups shelled sunflower seeds

½ cup sesame seeds

¾ cup unsalted peanuts *or* soy nuts

½ cup mini chocolate chips *or* snipped dried fruit, like apricots *or* apples

½ tsp. salt

1 cup honey

1 tsp. vanilla

1 cup peanut butter, smooth *or* crunchy

1. Grease the interior of the slow cooker crock well.

2. In a good-sized bowl, mix together coconut, dry oats, raisins or Craisins®, sunflower and sesame seeds, peanuts or soy nuts, chocolate chips or dried fruit, and salt.

3. In a separate bowl, blend together honey, vanilla, and peanut butter until smooth.

4. Add wet ingredients to dry ones, then grease your hands and use them to mix everything thoroughly.

5. Press the mixture firmly into the crock.

6. Cover. Bake on Low 2–3 hours, or until firm.

7. Uncover and set crock on baking rack to cool.

8. When room temperature, use a silicon or sturdy plastic knife to cut into 20 squares and 4 triangles.

9. Store in an airtight container.

TIP

Wrap a couple of these and carry them with you if you're going to be squeezed for breakfast or lunch. They'll give you energy for the day.

Viennese Walnut Bars

Makes 24 servings

Prep. Time: 30–35 minutes ❦ Cooking Time: 2½–3 hours

Ideal slow-cooker size: 6-quart oval

Pastry:

8 Tbsp. (1 stick) butter, softened

3-oz. pkg. cream cheese, softened

¼ cup sugar

1¼ cups flour

1 cup chopped walnuts

6-oz. pkg., or 1 cup, chocolate chips

Topping:

1 cup flour

¼ tsp. baking powder

¼ tsp. salt

1½ cups light brown sugar, packed

4 Tbsp. (half a stick) butter, softened

2 large eggs

1 tsp. instant coffee powder

1 Tbsp. hot water

½ cup chopped walnuts

1. Grease interior of slow cooker crock.

2. Make pastry by creaming together butter, cream cheese, and sugar.

3. Gradually beat in flour.

4. Press mixture evenly into bottom of crock.

5. Sprinkle with walnuts and chocolate chips.

6. Prepare topping by sifting flour, baking powder, and salt together into a medium-sized bowl.

7. Cream together brown sugar, butter, and eggs in a larger bowl.

8. Dissolve coffee in hot water. Add to creamed mixture.

9. Gradually add flour mixture to creamed.

10. Spoon over crust, spreading gently to cover.

11. Sprinkle with walnuts.

12. Cover. Bake on High 2½–3 hours, or until the topping firms up in the middle.

13. Carefully remove crock from cooker. Place on wire baking rack to cool.

14. When room temperature, cut bars into 20 squares and 4 triangles in the corners.

TIP

No, that teaspoon of coffee powder isn't a mistake. It brings a deep richness to the topping of these wonderful bars whose base is a rich shortbread. You will feel like you're on a plaza in a European city when you're eating these!

Raspberry Almond Bars

Makes 24 servings
Prep. Time: 20–30 minutes   ☙   Cooking Time: 2½–3 hours
Ideal slow-cooker size: 6-quart oval

1 cup flour
¾ cup quick dry oatmeal
½ cup sugar
8 Tbsp. (1 stick) butter, softened
½ tsp. almond extract
½ cup red raspberry preserves
⅓ cup sliced almonds

1. Grease interior of slow cooker crock.

2. In a large bowl, combine flour, oats, and sugar.

3. Cut in butter with a pastry cutter or two knives—or your fingers—until mixture forms coarse crumbs.

4. Stir in extract until well blended.

5. Set aside 1 cup crumbs.

6. Press remaining crumbs into bottom of crock.

7. Spread preserves over crust to within ½" of the edges (the preserves could burn if they touch the hot crock).

8. In a small bowl, combine reserved 1 cup crumbs with almonds. Sprinkle evenly over preserves, pressing down gently to hold the almonds in place.

9. Cover. Bake on High for 2½–3 hours, or until firm in center.

10. Uncover. Lift crock onto wire baking rack to cool.

11. When room temperature, cut bars into 20 squares and 4 triangles in the corners.

TIP
Watch for the raspberry preserves to ooze out around the edges as these bars bake!

Banana Pecan Bars

Makes 28 servings

Prep. Time: 20–30 minutes ❦ *Cooking Time: 2½–3 hours*
Ideal slow-cooker size: 6-quart oval

½ cup chopped pecans

2 cups flour

2 tsp. baking powder

⅛ tsp. cinnamon

2–3 very ripe bananas, enough to
make 1 cup when smooshed

¼ cup shortening at room
temperature

1 cup sugar

2 eggs

1 tsp. vanilla

Glaze:

½ lb. (rounded 1 cup)
confectioners sugar

1 tsp. rum extract

a shy 2 Tbsp. water *or*
orange juice

1. Grease interior of slow cooker crock.

2. Combine pecans, flour, baking powder, and cinnamon.

3. Using a fork, smoosh ripe bananas in a good-sized bowl, enough to equal 1 cup.

4. Cream shortening, sugar, and bananas together.

5. Stir in eggs and vanilla, mixing thoroughly.

6. Add dry ingredients to wet, stirring until just combined.

7. Spread batter into greased crock.

8. Cover. Bake on High 2–2½ hours, or until tester inserted in center of Bars comes out clean.

9. Uncover. Remove crock from cooker and place on wire baking rack to cool.

10. While bars are cooling, make glaze. Combine confectioners sugar and rum extract. Stir in just enough water or juice to make glaze pourable.

11. Drizzle glaze over bars. Then cut into 24 squares and 4 triangles in the corners.

Why I like this recipe—

I took these to a picnic potluck—
and they disappeared. They look
kind of bashful, but maybe it's
the rum extract in the glaze,
mixed with the aroma of bananas,
that draws attention.

Nutty Apricot Bars

Makes 24 servings

Prep. Time: 20 minutes ❦ Cooking Time 2–3 hours
Ideal slow-cooker size: 6-quart oval

2 eggs, *divided*

12 Tbsp. (1½ sticks) butter, softened and *divided*

1 tsp. baking powder

1 cup flour

1½ cups sugar, *divided*

1¼ cups quick oats

1 cup apricot jam *or* preserves

2 cups shredded coconut, sweetened *or* not

⅓ cup chopped pecans *or* walnuts

½ tsp. vanilla

1. Combine 1 egg, 8 Tbsp. (1 stick) softened butter, baking powder, flour, ¾ cup sugar, and quick oats until well mixed.

2. Grease interior of slow cooker crock.

3. Press batter into bottom of crock.

4. Spread batter with jam.

5. Mix together remaining egg, 4 Tbsp. (half a stick) softened butter, ¾ cup sugar, coconut, nuts, and vanilla.

6. Drop by spoonfuls over jam. Spread out to cover jam as best you can.

7. Cover. Bake on High for 2–3 hours, or until tester inserted into center of bars comes out clean.

8. Remove crock from cooker. Place, uncovered, on wire baking rack to cool.

9. When room temperature, use a silicone or plastic knife to cut bars into 20 squares, with 4 triangles in the corners.

TIP

Usually the lid of the cooker draws condensation—which you don't want to drip onto the bars or cakes that you're baking. So when you remove the lid, do a fast swoop, turning it quickly upside down away from yourself as you lift it off the cooker.

Frosty Lemon Bars

Makes 24 servings

Prep. Time: 20–30 minutes ❧ Cooking Time: 2½–3 hours
Ideal slow-cooker size: 6-quart oval

Crust:

2¼ cups flour

½ cup confectioners sugar

16 Tbsp. (2 sticks) butter, melted

Filling:

4 eggs

¼ cup lemon juice

2 cups white sugar

¼ cup flour

1 tsp. baking powder

3–4 Tbsp. confectioners sugar

Why I like this recipe—

It's the classic lemon bars, done in a slow cooker. Your kitchen has stayed cool, and you've been able to run a quick errand while they were baking.

1. Grease interior of slow cooker crock.

2. Prepare crust by combining flour and confectioners sugar in a good-sized mixing bowl.

3. Cut the butter into chunks. Work into dry ingredients with your hands until well blended.

4. Press mixture into bottom of crock.

5. Cover. Bake on High 1 hour.

6. Meanwhile, prepare filling. Beat eggs in the bowl where you made the crust.

7. Add lemon juice and mix well.

8. In a separate bowl, combine sugar, flour, and baking powder. Stir into wets and beat well.

9. Pour filling over crust.

10. Cover and bake on High 1½–2 more hours, or until filling sets up and is firm.

11. Uncover. Remove crock from cooker and place on wire baking rack to cool.

12. When bars have reached room temperature, sprinkle with confectioners sugar. Cut into 20 squares and 4 triangles.

13. Refrigerate until ready to serve.

Cherry Cheesecake Bars

Makes 24 servings
Prep. Time: 20–30 minutes ❦ *Cooking Time: 2½–3 hours*
Ideal slow-cooker size: 6-quart oval

Crust:

6 Tbsp. (¾ stick) butter, softened

½ cup light brown sugar, packed

1 cup flour

¾ cup toasted almonds

1 cup cherry preserves

Cheese Filling:

½ cup sugar

8-oz. pkg. cream cheese, softened and cut into chunks

1 egg

2 Tbsp. milk

½ tsp. almond extract

1. Grease interior of slow cooker crock.

2. Prepare crust by creaming together butter and brown sugar.

3. Blend in flour and almonds, by hand, until mixture is crumbly.

4. Set aside ½ cup crumbs.

5. Press remaining crumbs into bottom of crock.

6. Cover. Bake on High 1 hour.

7. Uncover. Remove crock from cooker and place on baking rack. Allow crust to cool while you mix up the filling.

8. Cream together sugar and cream cheese.

9. Blend in egg, milk, and almond extract.

10. Spread cherry preserves over crust.

11. Drop filling by spoonfuls over preserves. Spread filling out as well as you can without pulling up the preserves.

12. Sprinkle with reserved ½ cup crumbs.

13. Return crock to cooker. Cover. Continue cooking on High for 1½–2 hours, or until filling is set.

14. Uncover. Remove crock to baking rack to cool.

15. When bars are room temperature, cut into 20 squares and 4 triangles. Refrigerate until ready to serve.

TIP

You can do amazing things in a slow cooker, especially if you add ingredients in stages. The filling doesn't need to bake as long as the crust, so you add it later. You have the convenience of the slow cooker, but the ability to do more delicate dishes by staging the addition of ingredients that don't need to cook as long.

Crisps
and
Cobblers

Deep Dish Fruity Delight

Makes 12–15 servings
Prep. Time: 15 minutes ❧ *Cooking Time: 3½–4 hours*
Ideal slow-cooker size: 5- or 6-quart

20-oz. can crushed pineapple, drained

21-oz. can cherry, apple, *or* blueberry pie filling

18¼-oz. box yellow cake *or* angel food cake mix

8 Tbsp. (1 stick) butter, melted

½–1 cup chopped nuts

1. Grease interior of slow cooker crock.

2. Spread drained pineapple over bottom of crock.

3. Spoon pie filling evenly over pineapple.

4. Sprinkle dry cake mix over pie filling.

5. Drizzle melted butter over dry cake mix.

6. Sprinkle with nuts.

7. Cover. Bake on High 3½–4 hours, or until tester inserted into center of cobbler comes out clean.

8. Uncover, being careful not to let water from inside of lid drip on cobbler. Remove crock from cooker and place on wire baking rack to cool.

9. When warm or room temperature, slice or spoon out to serve.

A great variation—

Add 1 cup flaked or grated coconut to Step 6 if you wish.

Any-Fruit-That-Makes-You-Happy Cobbler

Makes 6–8 servings
Prep. Time: 15–20 minutes ❦ Cooking Time: 1½–3 hours
Ideal slow-cooker size: 3- or 5-quart

8 Tbsp. (1 stick) butter

1 cup flour

1 cup milk

1 cup sugar, *or less, depending on the sweetness of the fruit you're using*

2 tsp. baking powder

dash of salt

3–4 cups fresh fruit

A great variation—

Use whatever fruit is in season. Use more than is called for if you wish. You may need to cook it a bit longer, but this recipe is highly flexible.

1. Grease interior of slow cooker crock. This mixture will fit into 3-, 4-, and 5-quart cookers, whichever you have. The cobbler will be deeper in a 3-quart than in a 5-quart, if that matters to you.

2. Melt butter in a microwave-safe bowl. Stir in all other ingredients except fruit. Mix thoroughly.

3. Spoon batter into crock, spreading it out evenly.

4. Arrange cut-up fruit, pitted cherries, or berries on top of batter.

5. Cover. Bake on High 1½–3 hours, depending on the fruit. It's finished when the middle is set and juice is bubbling at the edges.

6. Uncover, being careful not to let the condensation on the interior of the cooker lid drip on the cobbler.

7. Let cool until it's the temperature you like.

Cobbler with Fresh Cherries

Makes 6 servings

Prep. Time: 20 minutes   ✣   Cooking Time: 2½–3½ hours   ✣   Standing Time: 1 hour
Ideal slow-cooker size: 4-quart

4 cups (about 2 lbs.) pitted fresh cherries, sweet *or* sour

⅓–¾ cup sugar, depending on how sweet the cherries are

1 Tbsp. instant tapioca

⅓ cup water

1 Tbsp. butter

Cobbler Batter:

8 Tbsp. (1 stick) butter

1¼ cups flour

1 cup sugar

2 Tbsp. baking powder

½ tsp. salt

1 cup milk

A great variation—

You can use canned or frozen cherries for this. If canned, cut the sugar back and use the juice instead of the water that's called for. I love sour cherries here because of the tart-sweet combination!

1. Grease interior of slow cooker crock.

2. In a good-sized saucepan, combine pitted cherries, the lesser amount of sugar, tapioca, and water.

3. Let stand for an hour, stirring now and then. Test the mixture to see if it's the sweetness you like. Now's the time to add more sugar if you want.

4. Cook over medium heat until boiling, stirring continually to prevent sticking and scorching. Simmer for 5–10 minutes stirring constantly.

5. Remove from heat. Stir in 1 Tbsp. butter.

6. To make batter, cut up stick of butter into slow cooker crock. Turn cooker onto High so butter melts.

7. Meanwhile, combine flour, sugar, baking powder, and salt in a good-sized bowl. When well mixed, stir in milk until batter is smooth.

8. Drop batter by spoonfuls evenly over melted butter in crock. Do not stir.

9. Spoon the thickened cherry mixture over batter. Do not stir.

10. Cover. Cook on High for 2–3 hours, or until firm in middle and bubbly around edges.

11. Remove lid carefully and swiftly so no drops of water from the lid drip onto the cobbler. Continue baking on High 30 more minutes so cobbler becomes drier on top.

12. Remove crock from cooker and place on baking rack to cool. When warm or room temperature, serve.

Peaches and Pudding Crisp

Makes 8 servings

Prep. Time: 20 minutes   ❧   Cooking Time: 3–4 hours
Ideal slow-cooker size: 5-quart

5–6 cups peaches,
fresh *or* canned

½ cup peach juice *or* syrup

2 small pkgs. instant vanilla
pudding, *divided*

½ cup brown sugar

Topping:

1 cup flour

1½ cups dry oatmeal,
quick *or* rolled

½ cup brown sugar

8 Tbsp. (1 stick) butter, melted

¾ tsp. salt

2 tsp. cinnamon

reserved dry instant vanilla
pudding

1. Grease interior of slow cooker crock.

2. Combine peaches, their syrup, 2 Tbsp. dry pudding mix, and brown sugar in good-sized mixing bowl. Set aside remaining dry pudding mix.

3. Place in slow cooker crock.

4. Combine all topping ingredients until well blended and crumbly. Sprinkle over peach mixture.

5. Cover. Bake on High 2½–3½ hours, or until firm in middle and bubbly around the edges.

6. Remove lid carefully, tilting it quickly away from yourself so that water from the inside of the lid doesn't drip on the crisp.

7. Continue baking 30 more minutes so crisp dries out on top.

8. Remove crock from cooker and place on baking rack to cool. Serve when warm or at room temperature.

TIP

I like the crisp to be crunchy, and it won't get brown on top in a slow cooker. So I like to run the finished dish under the broiler for just a minute or two til it's properly brown and crunchy. That, against the soft peaches—yum!

Peach Cobbler

Makes 8 servings
Prep. Time: 20 minutes ❧ Cooking Time: 3–4 hours
Ideal slow-cooker size: 5-quart

3–4 cups sliced peaches
⅓ cup sugar
¼ cup brown sugar
dash nutmeg
dash cinnamon
8 Tbsp. (1 stick) butter
½ cup sugar
¾ cup flour
2 tsp. baking powder
¾ cup milk

Some great variations—

*Love this in the summertime!
But it's also good with canned
or frozen peaches. Drain canned
peaches or thaw frozen ones
before adding them to the crock.
The cobbler won't firm up well
if you add that extra moisture.*

1. Grease interior of slow cooker crock.

2. Mix together in a good-sized bowl the peaches, ⅓ cup sugar, brown sugar, nutmeg, and cinnamon. Set aside to macerate.

3. Melt butter, or place in slow cooker crock turned on High, and let it melt there.

4. Meanwhile, stir together remaining ingredients in a bowl—½ cup sugar, flour, baking powder, and milk until smooth.

5. When butter is melted, make sure it covers the bottom of the crock. Spoon batter evenly over butter in crock, but don't stir.

6. Spoon sugared peaches over batter.

7. Cover. Bake on High 3–4 hours, or until firm in middle and bubbly around the edges.

8. Uncover carefully so condensation from inside of lid doesn't drip on the cobbler. Remove crock from cooker. Serve when warm with milk or ice cream.

Rhubarb Crunch

Makes 6–8 servings
Prep. Time: 30 minutes ❦ Cooking Time: 1½–2 hours
Ideal slow-cooker size: 3-quart

1 cup flour, sifted (use ½ cup whole wheat and ½ cup white if you wish)

¼ cup dry oats, quick *or* rolled

1 cup brown sugar, packed

8 Tbsp. butter (1 stick), melted

1 tsp. cinnamon

1 cup sugar

2 Tbsp. cornstarch

1 cup water

1 tsp. vanilla

2 cups diced rhubarb

1. In a good-sized bowl, stir together flour, dry oats, brown sugar, melted butter, and cinnamon until crumbly.

2. Set aside half the crumbs. Pat remaining crumbs over bottom of slow cooker crock.

3. Combine sugar, cornstarch, water, and vanilla in a 2-qt. microwave-safe bowl, stirring until smooth.

4. Add rhubarb to water/sugar mixture. Microwave, covered, on High for 2 minutes. Stir. Cook another minute, or until mixture becomes thick and clear, stirring frequently.

5. Pour rhubarb sauce over crumbs in crock.

6. Crumble remaining crumbs over top of sauce.

7. Cover. Bake on High 1 hour.

8. Uncover. (Make sure the lid doesn't drip water on top of crunch when removing it.) Bake on High an additional 30–60 minutes, or until crunch is crunchy on top.

9. Remove crock from cooker. Allow crunch to cool until it's warm or room temperature before digging in.

Why I like this recipe—
Tang-ily wonderful!

Strawberry Rhubarb Crisp

Makes 8 servings
Prep. Time: 30 minutes 🌱 Cooking Time: 3–4 hours
Ideal slow-cooker size: 5-quart

4 cups sliced rhubarb

4 cups sliced strawberries

¾ cup sugar

½ cup orange marmalade

3 Tbsp. flour

2 Tbsp. (¼ stick) butter, melted

Topping:

½ cup chopped nuts of your choice

¼ cup dry oats, quick *or* rolled

½ cup flour

1 tsp. cinnamon

6 Tbsp. (¾ cup) butter

1. Grease interior of slow cooker crock.

2. In a good-sized bowl, mix together sliced rhubarb and strawberries, sugar, orange marmalade, and flour.

3. Pour into crock.

4. Drizzle melted butter over fruit mixture.

5. In a separate bowl, make topping by mixing together chopped nuts, dry oats, flour, and cinnamon.

6. Blend butter into dry ingredients either with your fingers, 2 knives, or a pastry cutter until crumbs form.

7. Sprinkle crumbs evenly over fruit.

8. Cover cooker. Bake on High 2½–3½ hours, or until firm in middle and bubbly around edges.

9. Quickly remove lid, swooping it away from yourself so drops on inside of lid don't drip on the crisp. Continue baking 30 more minutes to allow crisp to dry on top.

10. Remove crock from cooker and place on wire baking rack to cool.

11. Serve crisp when warm or at room temperature.

A great variation—

Frozen strawberries are fine for this crisp—but I prefer to thaw them first and drain them well before adding them to the crock. The berries and rhubarb will still turn juicy as they bake.

Strawberry Crisp

Makes 6 servings
Prep. Time: 30 minutes 🌱 Cooking Time: 2½–3½ hours
Ideal slow-cooker size: 4-quart

I cup dry oats, quick *or* rolled
I cup flour
I cup brown sugar, packed
8 Tbsp. (I stick) butter
½ cup sugar, *or* less
4 cups sliced fresh strawberries

1. Grease interior of slow cooker crock.

2. In a good-sized bowl, combine dry oatmeal, flour, and brown sugar. Cut butter into chunks and work into dry ingredients with your fingers, 2 knives, or a pastry cutter until crumbly.

3. In a separate bowl, gently mix together sliced strawberries and sugar.

4. Divide crumbs in half. Place half into bottom of slow cooker crock. Press down to form crust.

5. Spoon strawberries evenly over crust.

6. Scatter remaining half of crumbs over strawberries.

7. Cover. Bake on High 2–3 hours, or until firm in center and bubbly around edges.

8. Remove lid carefully with a swift swoop away from yourself to keep condensation on inside of lid from dripping onto crisp. Continue baking on High another 30 minutes to allow crisp to dry on top.

9. Remove crock from cooker and place on wire baking rack to cool. Serve warm or at room temperature.

A great variation—

Frozen strawberries work in this recipe, too. It's best to let them thaw and then drain them well before spooning them over the crust.

Apricot Crisp

Makes 5 servings
Prep. Time: 20–30 minutes ❦ Cooking Time: 3½–4 hours
Ideal slow-cooker size: 4-quart

2¼ lbs. fresh apricots

1¼ cups flour

¼ cup chopped
walnuts *or* pecans

1¼ cups sugar

pinch ground cloves

pinch cardamom

1 tsp. cinnamon

12 Tbsp. (1½ sticks) butter

1. Grease interior of slow cooker crock.

2. Cut apricots in half, remove stone, and place fruit evenly into crock.

3. In a good-sized bowl, mix together flour, chopped nuts, sugar, cloves, cardamom, and cinnamon until well blended.

4. Cut butter into chunks. Using either your fingers, 2 knives, or a pastry cutter, work butter into dry ingredients.

5. When crumbly, scatter over apricot halves.

6. Cover. Bake on High 3–3½ hours, or until fruit is tender.

7. Remove lid carefully and quickly, tilting it away from yourself to prevent condensation on inside of lid from dripping onto crisp. Continue baking uncovered for another 30 minutes so crisp dries on top.

8. Remove crock and place on wire baking rack to cool. Serve crisp warm or at room temperature.

A great variation—

Try these with canned apricots, too. But drain them well before using. Cut the the sugar in half if the syrup is sweetened.

Fresh Plum Kuchen

Makes 6–8 servings
Prep. Time: 20 minutes ❧ Cooking Time: 2–3 hours
Ideal slow-cooker size 3- or 4-quart

4 Tbsp. (half a stick) butter, softened

¾ cup sugar

2 eggs

1 tsp. lemon zest

1 cup flour

1 tsp. baking powder

¼ cup milk

sugar

2 cups fresh plums (about 4 medium-sized ones)

1 Tbsp. cinnamon

½ cup brown sugar

1. In a mixing bowl, beat butter and sugar together until light and creamy.

2. Beat in the eggs and lemon zest.

3. In a separate bowl, combine flour and baking powder.

4. Add dry ingredients to wet. Add milk, mixing well.

5. Grease interior of slow cooker crock.

6. Sprinkle bottom and sides of crock lightly with sugar.

7. Spoon in batter, spreading it out evenly.

8. Slice plums and arrange on top of dough.

9. In dry ingredient bowl, stir cinnamon and brown sugar together. Sprinkle over plums.

10. Cover with slow cooker lid. Bake on High 2–3 hours, until middle is set and juice is bubbling.

11. Remove lid with a big swoop away from yourself to prevent condensation on inside of lid from dripping onto the kuchen.

12. Lift crock out of cooker and let kuchen cool until warm or room temperature before eating.

TIP

It's not a bad idea to keep a fresh lemon in your fridge all the time. Then you can add a teaspoon of zest to a dessert like this one. You'll start to see possibilities for using fresh lemon juice in salad dressings or grating zest over roasted pork and grilled beef. Or add slices of lemon to your drinking water any time.

Blueberry Crinkle

Makes 6–8 servings
Prep. Time: 15–20 minutes ❦ *Cooking Time: 2–3 hours*
Ideal slow-cooker size: 3- or 4-quart

½ cup brown sugar

¾ cup dry quick oats

½ cup flour,
white *or* whole wheat

½ tsp. cinnamon

dash of salt

6 Tbsp. (¾ stick) butter

4 cups blueberries,
fresh *or* frozen

2 Tbsp. sugar

2 Tbsp. instant tapioca

2 Tbsp. lemon juice

½ tsp. lemon zest

1. Grease interior of slow cooker crock.

2. In a large bowl, combine brown sugar, dry oats, flour, cinnamon, and salt.

3. Using 2 knives, a pastry cutter, or your fingers, work butter into dry ingredients until small crumbs form.

4. In a separate bowl, stir together blueberries, sugar, tapioca, lemon juice, and lemon zest.

5. Spoon blueberry mixture into slow cooker crock.

6. Sprinkle crumbs over blueberries.

7. Cover. Cook 2–3 hours on Low, or until firm in the middle with juice bubbling up around the edges.

8. Remove lid with a giant swoop away from yourself so condensation on inside of lid doesn't drip on the crumbs.

9. Lift crock out of cooker. Let cool until either warm or room temperature before eating.

A great variation—

When blueberries are in season, I buy a 13-lb. box, pour the berries into pint-sized containers, and freeze them. No need to thaw them for this recipe. Of course, fresh can't be beat in this crinkle. My latest craze is to eat this with dollops of Greek yogurt.

Old-Timey Raisin Crisp

Makes 12 servings

Prep. Time: 20 minutes ❦ *Cooking Time: 2½–3½ hours* ❦ *Standing Time: 1 hour*
Ideal slow-cooker size: 5-quart

1 lb. raisins

2 Tbsp. cornstarch

½ cup sugar

1 cup water

2 Tbsp. lemon juice

Crumbs:

1¾ cups flour

½ tsp. baking soda

1 cup brown sugar

¼ tsp. salt

1½ cups dry oats, quick *or* rolled

12 Tbsp. (1½ sticks) butter

1. Grease interior of slow cooker crock.

2. In a saucepan, combine raisins, cornstarch, sugar, and water. Cook until slightly thickened, stirring continually.

3. Remove from heat, stir in lemon juice and let cool for an hour.

4. Prepare crumbs by combining flour, baking soda, brown sugar, salt, and dry oats in a good-sized bowl until well mixed.

5. Cut butter into chunks. Work into dry ingredients with your fingers, 2 knives, or a pastry cutter until fine crumbs form.

6. Divide crumbs in half. Spread half into bottom of slow cooker crock. Press down to form crust.

7. Spoon raisin mixture over crumb crust.

8. Cover with remaining half of crumbs.

9. Cover. Bake on High 2–3 hours, or until firm in middle and bubbly around the edges.

10. Remove lid carefully and quickly so drops of water from inside the lid don't drip on the crisp.

11. Continue baking 30 more minutes to allow the crisp to dry on top.

12. Remove crock from cooker and place on baking rack.

13. Cut into squares, or spoon out of crock, to serve when warm or at room temperature.

Why I like this recipe—
This recipe makes me think of Grandma because she loved raisin desserts. They were always available, and she had quite a line-up of raisin dishes.

TIP

Don't skip the lemon juice. It makes sure the crisp isn't super-sweet. Add a little more if you'd like to really taste it.

Spicy Sweet Apple Crisp

Makes 6 servings
Prep. Time: 20 minutes   ❧   Cooking Time: 3½–4 hours
Ideal slow-cooker size: 5-quart

9 crisp baking apples,
peeled *or* not

I cup flour

I cup sugar

I tsp. baking powder

pinch of salt

I egg

4 Tbsp. (half a stick) butter

several shakes of
roasted, *or* other gourmet,
cinnamon

dash *or* two of cardamom

1. Grease interior of slow cooker crock.

2. Slice apples into crock, spreading them out evenly.

3. In a good-sized bowl, mix together flour, sugar, baking powder, and salt.

4. Break egg into dry ingredients and mix together.

5. Cut butter into chunks. Using your fingers, or 2 knives, or a pastry cutter, work into dough until small chunks form.

6. Scatter chunks over apples.

7. Sprinkle liberally with roasted cinnamon. Add a dash or two of cardamom.

8. Cover with cooker lid. Bake on High 3–3½ hours, or until firm in the middle and juices bubble up around the edges.

9. Remove lid carefully, tilting it quickly away from yourself so no condensation drips on the crisp. Continue baking 30 more minutes to allow the topping to crisp up.

10. Let cool until warm or room temperature before serving.

Why I like this recipe—

If you'd like to shake up the traditional apple crisp just a little bit, this is a winner.

Apple Pear Crisp

Makes 8–10 servings
Prep. Time: 15–20 minutes ❧ Cooking Time: 2–4 hours
Ideal slow-cooker size: 5-quart

3–4 large apples, unpeeled and
sliced

3–4 large pears, unpeeled and
sliced

½ cup sugar, *or less, depending
on how naturally sweet the
apples are*

I Tbsp. lemon juice

I Tbsp. flour

Topping:

I cup flour

I cup brown sugar

⅔ cup dry oats, quick or rolled
(rolled have more texture)

½ tsp. cinnamon

6 Tbsp. (¾ stick) butter

1. Grease interior of slow cooker crock.

2. In a big bowl, mix together apple and pear slices, sugar, lemon juice, and 1 Tbsp. flour.

3. Pour into crock.

4. In the same bowl, mix topping ingredients: flour, brown sugar, dry oats, and cinnamon. Then cut in butter with 2 knives, a pastry cutter, or your fingers. When crumbs the size of small peas form, sprinkle over fruit mixture.

5. Cover crock. Bake on High 2–3 hours, or on Low 4 hours, or until fruit is bubbly.

6. Thirty minutes before end of cooking time, remove lid (don't let condensation from inside of lid drip on the crisp), so the topping can dry.

7. Serve as is, or topped with ice cream or in a bowl with milk.

Why I like this recipe—

This is year-round versatile. We eat it for breakfast, for a quick supper, or for a late afternoon or evening snack if we haven't had a substantial lunch or dinner. It's delicious warm or cold.

Puddings
and
Custards

Banana Bread Pudding with Butterscotch Sauce

Makes 10 servings

Prep. Time: 30 minutes ❧ *Cooking Time: 2–3 hours* ❧ *Standing Time: 10 minutes*
Ideal slow-cooker size: 5-quart

5 ripe bananas, peeled and sliced in coins

10 cups diced white French bread, stale

5 eggs

3½ cups whole milk

¾ cup brown sugar, *divided*

¼ tsp. ground nutmeg

¾ tsp. salt, *divided*

2 tsp. vanilla, *divided*

2 Tbsp. dark spiced rum, *divided*

4 Tbsp. (½ stick) salted butter

½ cup heavy cream

1. In a greased slow cooker, make 2 or 3 layers of banana slices and bread, starting with banana slices.

2. In a mixing bowl, whisk eggs until they no longer cling to the whisk.

3. Add milk, ¼ cup brown sugar, nutmeg, ½ tsp. salt, 1 tsp. vanilla, and 1 Tbsp. rum.

4. Pour milk mixture gently over layers in crock. Be sure bread cubes are submerged.

5. Cover and cook on High for 2–3 hours, until bread pudding is set in the middle and edges are browning.

6. Set aside with lid off to firm up while you make the butterscotch sauce. The puffiness will sink down a bit.

7. In a medium saucepan, combine butter, remaining ½ cup brown sugar, cream, remaining ¼ tsp. salt, and remaining 1 Tbsp. rum.

8. Cook and stir over medium heat until sauce is just coming to a gentle boil. Lower heat to keep at a low boil for 5 minutes, stirring occasionally.

9. Add remaining 1 tsp. vanilla to sauce. Serve warm over warm bread pudding.

TIP

I use this butterscotch sauce for other desserts as well—ice cream, tapioca pudding, plain chocolate cake, and so on. Keep it in the fridge and warm it slightly before using so you can stir and recombine the sauce. However, I sometimes stick a spoon in the cold sauce and just take a luxurious mouthful when no one is looking. . . .

Apple Walnut Bread Pudding with Whiskey Sauce

Makes 10 servings

Prep. Time: 30 minutes ❦ *Cooking Time: 2–3 hours* ❦ *Standing Time: 30 minutes*
Ideal slow-cooker size: 5-quart

10 cups diced stale bread, a mixture of kinds is fine

2 cups peeled, chopped apples

5 eggs

3½ cups whole milk

½ cup brown sugar, *divided*

1 tsp. ground cinnamon

½ tsp. vanilla

½ tsp. salt

½ cup chopped walnuts, toasted

3 Tbsp. salted butter

¼ cup heavy cream

2 Tbsp. whiskey

1. Place half the bread in a greased slow cooker. Add all the apples as a layer. Cover with remaining bread.

2. In a mixing bowl, whisk eggs until they no longer cling to the whisk. Add milk, ¼ cup brown sugar, cinnamon, vanilla, and salt.

3. Pour milk mixture gently over layers in crock. Push bread cubes down so they are completely submerged.

4. Cover and cook on High for 2–3 hours until slightly puffy and liquid is absorbed.

5. Sprinkle with walnuts, pressing gently into the tender top.

6. Set aside with lid off to firm up while you make the whiskey sauce. Expect the puff to sink down as the pudding sits.

7. In a saucepan, combine butter, remaining ¼ cup brown sugar, cream, and whiskey.

8. Stir and cook over medium heat until it reaches a gentle boil. Remove from heat and serve warm over warm bread pudding.

Chocolate Bread Pudding

Makes 10 servings
Prep. Time: 15 minutes   ❦   Cooking Time: 2–3 hours
Ideal slow-cooker size: 5-quart

1 Tbsp. butter

10 cups cubed white bread, preferably hearty and preferably stale

3½ cups whole milk

5 eggs

2 tsp. vanilla

¼ cup sugar

½ cup brown sugar

3 Tbsp. unsweetened cocoa powder

½ cup semisweet chocolate chips

1. Grease slow cooker with butter.

2. Place bread cubes in buttered slow cooker.

3. In a mixing bowl, beat together milk, eggs, and vanilla. Add both sugars and cocoa. Whisk again.

4. Pour milk mixture over bread. Push any floating cubes down into the mixture.

5. Sprinkle with chocolate chips.

6. Cover and cook on High for 2–3 hours until puffy and liquid is absorbed.

7. Serve hot, warm, or chilled. The puffiness will subside as the pudding cools.

TIP

Stale, or even toasted, bread makes a better texture in bread pudding. It soaks up the custard more nicely and gives a better flavor. If you're starting with fresh bread, either allow it to sit uncovered at room temperature overnight, or toast it lightly. Serve with caramel sauce or fresh berries.

Classic Bread Pudding

Makes 10 servings

Prep. Time: 25 minutes ❦ Cooking Time: 2–3 hours

Ideal slow-cooker size: 5-quart

4 Tbsp. (½ stick) butter, melted

10 cups diced white bread, stale

⅔ cup raisins

5 eggs

3½ cups whole milk

⅓ cup sugar

½ tsp. vanilla

1 tsp. cinnamon

½ tsp. salt

1. Pour butter in slow cooker and swirl it around to grease the bottom and up the sides several inches.

2. Add bread cubes and raisins to slow cooker. Mix gently.

3. In a mixing bowl, whisk eggs until they no longer cling to the whisk. Add milk, sugar, vanilla, cinnamon, and salt.

4. Pour milk mixture over bread mixture. Push floating cubes down into the mixture so they get a coating.

5. Cover and cook on High for 2–3 hours, until liquid is absorbed and the pudding is puffy and browning at the edges.

6. Serve hot, warm, or chilled. Expect the puff to sink down as the pudding cools.

Why I like this recipe—

"Pudding" seems like a strange name for this comforting dessert. It's like a fudgy pudding, really, with the bread turning into something tender and yet substantial as it bakes. Eat classic bread pudding as it is, or serve a caramel sauce and fruit on top.

Breakfast Cornbread Pudding

Makes 10 servings
Prep. Time: 25 minutes   ❦   Cooking Time: 2–3 hours
Ideal slow-cooker size: 6-quart

4 Tbsp. (½ stick) butter, *divided*

5 cups cubed cornbread, toasted

5 cups cubed bread

1 cup cooked, crumbled country sausage

2 green onions, diced

¼ cup chopped red bell pepper

½ cup corn

4 cups whole milk

6 eggs

¼ tsp. dried thyme

½ tsp. salt

pepper, to taste

1. Use 1 Tbsp. butter to grease slow cooker.

2. In the slow cooker, gently stir together cornbread, bread, sausage, onions, peppers, and corn.

3. In a mixing bowl, whisk together milk, eggs, thyme, salt, and pepper.

4. Pour milk mixture over bread mixture, pushing down on bread as needed so it is submerged.

5. Melt remaining 3 Tbsp. butter and drizzle over top.

6. Cover and cook on High for 2–3 hours, until liquid is absorbed and pudding is puffy. Serve hot or warm (although the puffiness will sink down as pudding sits).

Why I like this recipe—

This is a tasty twist on the traditional breakfast casserole. The cornbread gives excellent flavor and texture and it's a handy way to use up leftover cornbread.

Pumpkin Custard

Makes 6 servings
Prep. Time: 15 minutes ❦ *Cooking Time: 2–3 hours*
Ideal slow-cooker size: 3-quart

1 Tbsp. butter

1½ cups cooked, pureed pumpkin

⅔ cup dark brown sugar

3 eggs, beaten

1 cup heavy cream

1 Tbsp. flour

1 tsp. ground cinnamon

½ tsp. ground ginger

½ tsp. ground nutmeg

¼ tsp. ground cloves

½ tsp. salt

1. Use butter to grease slow cooker.

2. Combine rest of ingredients, whisking well.

3. Pour into buttered crock.

4. Cover and cook on High for 2–3 hours until set in the middle. Serve warm.

TIP

Make this into a pumpkin pie by lining a 6-quart oval crock with pastry for a 9" pie. Bring the pastry up the sides 1–2". Pour in the custard. Cover and cook on High for 2–3 hours until set. Allow to cool for easier slicing and serving.

Raspberry Custard

Makes 6 servings

Prep. Time: 15 minutes ❦ Cooking Time: 3–4 hours ❦ Standing Time: 30–60 minutes
Ideal slow-cooker size: 4-quart

5 eggs

½ cup sugar

½ tsp. salt

¾ cup all-purpose flour

12-oz. can evaporated milk

1 tsp. vanilla extract

pinch cinnamon

2 Tbsp. butter

2 cups red raspberries, fresh *or* frozen, thawed and drained

1. Beat eggs, sugar, and salt in mixing bowl until eggs no longer cling to whisk.

2. Add flour in three portions, whisking well after each addition until no lumps remain.

3. Whisk in evaporated milk, vanilla, and cinnamon.

4. Use butter to generously grease slow cooker.

5. Pour egg mixture into cooker. Sprinkle evenly with raspberries.

6. Cover and cook on Low for 3–4 hours, until set.

7. Remove lid and allow to cool for 30–60 minutes before serving. May chill before serving as well.

A great variation—

Of course you can use other berries in this custard, whatever you have in the freezer or find to pick.

Spanish Flan

Makes 6 servings
Prep. Time: 20 minutes ❧ *Cooking Time: 3–5 hours*
Ideal slow-cooker size: 5-quart

1 cup sugar

¼ tsp. lemon juice

3 eggs

14-oz. can sweetened condensed milk

12-oz. can evaporated milk

1 tsp. vanilla

pinch salt

1. Place sugar and lemon juice in slow cooker.

2. With lid off, cook on High for 1–2 hours, occasionally tilting the slow cooker to move sugar around as it caramelizes. When the sugar has browned into liquid caramel, turn setting to Low.

3. In a mixing bowl, whisk together eggs, both milks, vanilla, and salt.

4. Pour gently and evenly over caramel in slow cooker.

5. Cover and cook on Low for an additional 2–3 hours until set.

6. Remove lid from cooker and allow flan to cool for 30 minutes.

7. Run a knife around the edge of the flan. Invert crock over rimmed platter. Caramel should pool around the edges of the flan. Cut into slices and serve with extra caramel drizzled on top.

TIP

This is an easy way to caramelize sugar: let the slow cooker do it for you!

Maple Pot de Creme

Makes 4–6 servings
Prep. Time: 10 minutes ❧ *Cooking Time: 2–3 hours*
Chilling Time: at least 2 hours ❧ *Standing Time: about 1 hour*
Ideal slow-cooker size: 6-quart

2 egg yolks

2 eggs

1 cup heavy cream

½ cup whole milk

1 Tbsp. dark brown sugar

⅓ cup grade B (dark) maple syrup

pinch salt

1 tsp. vanilla

¼ tsp. ground nutmeg

whipped cream, for garnish, *optional*

1. In a mixing bowl, beat egg yolks and eggs until light and frothy.

2. Add cream, milk, brown sugar, maple syrup, salt, vanilla, and nutmeg. Mix well.

3. Use a baking dish that fits in your slow cooker.

4. Pour maple mixture in baking dish and set it in slow cooker.

5. Carefully pour water around the baking dish until the water comes halfway up the sides.

6. Cover cooker. Cook on High for 2–3 hours, until pot de creme is set but still a little bit jiggly in the middle.

7. Wearing oven mitts to protect your knuckles, carefully remove hot dish from cooker. Set on wire rack to cool to room temperature.

8. Cover tightly and chill for at least 2 hours before serving. Garnish with whipped cream if you wish.

Why I like this recipe—

Want an impressive, special dessert with very little effort? This is it! The texture is luscious, the flavor is delightful, and you can dress it up with whipped cream and berries or a drizzle of chocolate sauce.

Simple Egg Custard

Makes 6 servings

Prep. Time: 20 minutes ❦ *Cooking Time: 2–3 hours* ❦ *Chilling Time: 4 hours*
Ideal slow-cooker size: 6-quart

2 cups whole milk

4 eggs

⅓ cup sugar

½ tsp. salt

1 tsp. vanilla

1. Place ingredients in blender. Whip well.

2. Divide between 4–6 ramekins, or 6 ¼ pint canning jars.

3. Space the ramekins/jars out in slow cooker.

4. Pour water in slow cooker, being careful to avoid ramekins, so water comes up halfway up the sides of the ramekins.

5. Cover and cook on High for 2–3 hours, until custard is set.

6. Carefully remove hot ramekins from slow cooker—a canning jar lifter works perfectly for this—and set on wire rack to cool to room temperature. Chill, covered, for at least 4 hours before serving.

TIP

If you can get your hands on really nice eggs with the deep yellow-orange yolks (usually straight from the farm!), your custard will show that lovely buttery color. But of course, any eggs will work.

TIP

If you use ¼ pint canning jars for making this recipe, you can easily take this delicious dessert with you. Just screw on a canning lid and ring and go! Perfect for picnics and packed lunches.

A great variation—

Add a few berries or some sliced peaches in the bottom of the ramekins before pouring in the egg/milk mixture.

Crockery Chocolate Pudding

Makes 4 servings

Prep. Time: 15 minutes ❦ *Cooking Time: 3–4 hours* ❦ *Chilling Time: 4 hours*
Ideal slow-cooker size: 3-quart

½ cup sugar

3 Tbsp. cornstarch

3 Tbsp. unsweetened cocoa powder

1 cup half-and-half

1¼ cups milk

1 tsp. vanilla

1 Tbsp. salted butter

1. Combine all ingredients in greased slow cooker. Whisk well.

2. Cover and cook on Low for 3–4 hours, whisking thoroughly twice, until pudding is thickened.

3. Pour into serving dish and chill at least 4 hours, covered, before serving.

A great variation—

If you prefer a less sweet pudding, use ⅓ cup sugar.

Tropical Pineapple Pudding

Makes 8 servings

Prep. Time: 15 minutes ❦ *Cooking Time: 3–4 hours*
Ideal slow-cooker size: 3-quart

20-oz. can crushed pineapple,
undrained

11-oz. can mandarin oranges,
undrained

2 eggs, beaten

½ cup coconut milk

3 Tbsp. cornstarch

½ cup sugar

¼ tsp. salt

zest and juice of 1 lime

toasted grated coconut, *optional*,
for garnish

1. Combine pineapple and oranges in slow cooker.

2. Separately, whisk eggs, coconut milk, cornstarch, sugar, salt, lime zest, and lime juice until totally smooth.

3. Add egg mixture to fruit in slow cooker, mixing to combine thoroughly.

4. Cover and cook on Low for 3–4 hours, whisking thoroughly twice, until thick.

5. Allow to sit with lid off for 30 minutes before serving warm. Or transfer to serving dish and chill for several hours in fridge before serving.

A great variation—

Make tropical parfaits by layering chilled pudding in pretty glasses with vanilla wafers or similar cookies, whipped cream, toasted grated coconut, and sliced bananas.

Vanilla Bean Rice Pudding

Makes 8 servings
Prep. Time: 20 minutes ❧ Cooking Time: 2–4 hours
Ideal slow-cooker size: 4-quart

6 cups milk, 2% *or* whole

1 ½ cups white rice, uncooked

1 cup sugar

2 Tbsp. butter, melted

½ tsp. salt

½ tsp. ground cinnamon

1 vanilla bean

1 egg

1. Combine milk, rice, sugar, butter, salt, and cinnamon in slow cooker.

2. Split vanilla bean in half and scrape seeds into milk mixture. Drop in split bean as well.

3. Cover and cook on High for 2–4 hours, until rice is tender and most of the milk is absorbed.

4. Whisk egg in a small bowl.

5. Slowly add ½ cup hot rice mixture to beaten egg, whisking constantly.

6. Slowly pour rice/egg mixture back into slow cooker, whisking constantly. Whisk an additional minute.

7. Cover and allow to stand 10 minutes.

8. Pour hot pudding into serving dish. Serve warm, or chill first before serving.

A great variation—

Add 1 cup raisins in step 1.

TIP

Steps 4–6 are called "tempering" the egg. This gentle introduction of the egg to the hot pudding helps to thicken the pudding while keeping the silky texture of the egg. Putting the egg straight into hot pudding would create scrambled egg!

Raspberrioca

Makes 8–10 servings
Prep. Time: 10 minutes ❦ *Cooking Time: 3–6 hours* ❦ *Chilling Time: 2 or more hours*
Ideal slow-cooker size: 3-quart

4 cups water
½ cup pearl tapioca
3-oz. box raspberry gelatin
⅓ cup sugar
2 cups frozen red raspberries
1 cup heavy whipping cream

1. In slow cooker, combine water and tapioca.

2. Cover and cook on Low for 6 hours or High for 3 hours, stirring twice.

3. Stir in gelatin and sugar until dissolved.

4. Gently stir in raspberries.

5. Pour into bowl and refrigerate until chilled.

6. Use an electric mixer to beat cream into soft peaks in chilled bowl. Stir into chilled tapioca. Serve.

Why I like this recipe—

This is a lovely, refreshing pink cloud in the summer. I have used other berries with success as well.

Vanilla Tapioca

Makes 8 servings

Prep. Time: 5 minutes ❦ Cooking time: 3–6 hours ❦ Standing Time: 30 minutes

Ideal slow-cooker size: 3- or 4-quart

4 cups milk, preferably 2%

2 eggs

⅔ cup sugar

½ cup pearl tapioca

¼ tsp. salt

1 tsp. vanilla

1. In slow cooker, whisk milk and eggs together until eggs no longer cling to whisk.

2. Add sugar, tapioca, and salt. Mix again.

3. Cover and cook on Low for 6 hours or on High for 3 hours, whisking thoroughly twice.

4. Add vanilla.

5. Remove crock from electric cooker and allow to sit uncovered for 30 minutes before serving warm. Alternatively, transfer pudding to serving dish and refrigerate for several hours before serving cold.

TIP

Great with fresh fruit on top, or any toppings you enjoy on ice cream.

Strawberry Rhubarb Sauce

Makes 6 servings
Prep. Time: 20 minutes ❦ Cooking Time: 3–4 hours
Chilling Time: 2 hours ❦ Standing Time: 1 hour
Ideal slow-cooker size: 4-quart

1½ lbs. rhubarb, cut in ½" pieces

pinch salt

⅓ cup water

½ cup sugar

2 cups diced strawberries

1. Combine rhubarb, salt, water, and sugar in slow cooker.

2. Cover and cook on Low for 3–4 hours.

3. Pour sauce into serving dish. Allow to cool to room temperature.

4. Stir strawberries gently into sauce. Chill at least 2 hours before serving.

TIP

Serve as is in small dessert dishes, or serve as a sauce over pound cake, angel food cake, or ice cream.

Mocha Pie

Makes 8 servings

Prep. Time: 20 minutes ❦ *Cooking Time: 2–3 hours* ❦ *Standing Time: 2 hours*
Ideal slow-cooker size: 6-quart

crust for a 9" pie

2 eggs

⅔ cup heavy whipping cream

1½ cups sugar

3 Tbsp. unsweetened cocoa
powder

1 Tbsp. instant coffee granules

4 Tbsp. (½ stick) butter, melted

1 tsp. vanilla

¼ tsp. salt

1. Take rolled out pastry and fit it into slow cooker as you would line a pie plate, bringing it up the sides 1–2" and gently pushing it into the bottom.

2. In a mixing bowl, beat eggs and cream until mixture no longer clings to whisk.

3. Add rest of ingredients and whisk well.

4. Pour filling into prepared crust.

5. Cover and cook on High for 2–3 hours, until filling is set in the middle and crust is browning.

6. Remove crock from electrical unit, uncover, and set aside to cool for 2 hours before slicing and serving.

Some great variations—

I adore chocolate and coffee together, so this pie is a favorite of mine. However, I bet there are ways to tinker with it: take out the coffee, and put a layer of peanut butter between the filling and the crust. . . add some cinnamon and cayenne for a Mexican flair. . . or chop up some leftover Halloween candy bars and sprinkle them in the crust before pouring in the filling.

Chocolate Pecan Pie

Makes 8 servings

Prep. Time: 25 minutes   ❧   Cooking Time: 2–3 hours   ❧   Standing Time: 30–60 minutes

Ideal slow-cooker size: 6-quart

pastry for a 9" pie

6-oz. bag chopped pecans, about 1⅓ cups

4 oz. bittersweet chocolate, chopped

3 eggs

1 cup sugar

6 Tbsp. butter, melted

½ cup dark corn syrup

¼ cup maple syrup

1 tsp. vanilla

¼ tsp. salt

1. Take rolled out pastry and fit it into slow cooker as you would line a pie plate, bringing it up the sides 1–2" and gently pushing it into the bottom.

2. In a small bowl, toss together chocolate and pecans. Sprinkle evenly in pie crust.

3. In a medium bowl, whisk eggs and sugar. Add butter, corn syrup, maple syrup, vanilla, and salt. Whisk again.

4. Pour filling over chocolate/pecans in crust.

5. Cover and cook on High for 2–3 hours, until filling is set and crust is getting browned.

6. Remove crock from electrical unit, remove lid, and set pie aside to cool to room temperature, about 2 hours, before slicing and serving.

Why I like this recipe—

Although this is a particularly decadent, delicious pie, it is very easy to make. It's a favorite of my extended family for holiday gatherings.

Famous PA Dutch Shoofly Pie

Makes 8 servings

Prep. Time: 30 minutes   ❧   Cooking Time: 1½–2 hours   ❧   Standing Time: 30–60 minutes

Ideal slow-cooker size: 6-quart

pastry for a 9" pie

1 cup all-purpose flour

½ cup brown sugar

2 Tbsp. butter, room temperature

⅓ cup blackstrap molasses

⅔ cup mild baking molasses

1 egg

⅔ cup cold water

1 tsp. baking soda

¼ cup hot water

Why I like this recipe—
We love this pie the traditional Pennsylvania Dutch way: for breakfast! But it's also delicious with a glass of cold milk and a peach on the side in the middle of summer.

1. Take rolled out pastry and fit it into slow cooker as you would line a pie plate, bringing it up the sides 2" and gently pushing it into the bottom.

2. In a mixing bowl, cut together flour, brown sugar, and butter to make fine crumbs. Measure and set aside ½ cup crumbs.

3. In another mixing bowl, combine both molasses, egg, and cold water. Whisk.

4. Separately, dissolve baking soda in hot water and then add it to mixture. Whisk again.

5. Add crumbs to molasses mixture. Pour into pie shell in cooker. Sprinkle with reserved ½ cup crumbs.

6. Cover, adding 3–4 sheets of paper towels under the lid to catch condensation.

7. Cook on High for 1½–2 hours, until pie is puffed a bit and center is not jiggly.

8. Uncover slow cooker and remove crock from electrical unit. Set aside for 30–60 minutes before slicing and serving pie.

Magic Coconut Custard Pie

Makes 8 servings

Prep. Time: 10 minutes ❧ *Cooking Time: 2–3 hours* ❧ *Standing Time: 30–60 minutes*
Ideal slow-cooker size: 5-quart

4 eggs

6 Tbsp. butter, room temperature

½ cup all-purpose flour

2 cups 2% or whole milk

¾ cup sugar

1 tsp. vanilla

1 cup unsweetened shredded coconut

1. In a blender, combine eggs, butter, flour, milk, sugar, and vanilla. Whip.

2. Stir in coconut.

3. Pour mixture into greased slow cooker.

4. Cover and cook on High for 2–3 hours, until set in the middle.

5. Uncover slow cooker and remove crock from electrical unit. Set aside for 30–60 minutes before slicing and serving pie, or allow to cool to room temperature for a totally firm pie.

Why I like this recipe—

The "magic" here is that the pie forms its own crust! I like to serve slices of this pie with some fresh berries or fruit salad.

Double-Crust Cherry Pie

Makes 8 servings

Prep. Time: 20 minutes ❦ *Cooking Time: 1½–2 hours* ❦ *Standing Time: 30–60 minutes*
Ideal slow-cooker size: 6-quart

2 21-oz. cans cherry pie filling

1 tsp. almond extract

crust for 2 9" pies

1. Take one of the rolled out pastries and fit it into slow cooker as you would line a pie plate, bringing it up the sides 1–2" and gently pushing it into the bottom.

2. Separately, stir together pie filling and almond extract. Spoon into crust in slow cooker.

3. Cut remaining crust in 1" strips. Lay half the strips ½" apart on top of the pie filling, pinching the ends gently to the bottom crust and removing excess length. Lay the rest of the strips the opposite direction in the same manner.

4. Cover and cook on High for 1½–2 hours, until crust is firm and getting brown and filling is hot.

5. Remove hot crock from electrical unit and set aside to cool for 30–60 minutes before cutting. For a totally firm pie, allow to cool to room temperature before serving.

Why I like this recipe—

This is it: the American classic! Cherry pie is a classic because it's straightforward and delicious, especially served with vanilla ice cream. Sometimes I just can't resist and I put triple-chocolate ice cream on my slice. Definitely special!

Open-Face Peach Pie

Makes 8 servings

Prep. Time: 30 minutes   ❧   Cooking Time: 1½–2 hours   ❧   Standing Time: 30–60 minutes
Ideal slow-cooker size: 6-quart

1 cup all-purpose flour

⅓ cup whole wheat flour

¼ tsp. baking powder

½ tsp. salt

2 Tbsp. confectioners sugar

4 Tbsp. (½ stick) butter, room temperature

3 cups sliced fresh peaches, any juice drained off

¼ cup sugar

1 tsp. ground cinnamon

1 egg

1 cup plain Greek yogurt

1. In a mixing bowl, combine both flours, baking powder, salt, and confectioners sugar. Cut in butter with a pastry cutter or 2 knives to make fine crumbs.

2. Press crumb mixture in slow cooker to make crust that covers bottom and comes up 1–2" on the sides.

3. Distribute peaches over crust. Sprinkle evenly with sugar and cinnamon.

4. In a small mixing bowl, beat egg. Add yogurt and stir.

5. Pour yogurt mixture evenly over peaches.

6. Cover and cook on High for 1½–2½ hours, until yogurt topping is firm and crust is slightly browned.

7. Carefully remove hot crock from electrical unit and remove lid. Allow pie to rest for 30–60 minutes before cutting and serving. For a totally firm pie, allow to cool to room temperature.

TIP
You may use canned peaches in place of fresh ones, but drain them very well.

Why I like this recipe—
This pie is similar to one my mother made when I was a child. I love the refreshing flavors of peach and yogurt together.

Blueberry Ginger Tart

Makes 8 servings

Prep. Time: 30 minutes ❦ *Cooking Time: 1½–2 hours* ❦ *Standing Time: 30–60 minutes*
Ideal slow-cooker size: 6-quart

1 cup whole wheat pastry flour

¾ cup all-purpose flour

¼ cup brown sugar

⅛ tsp. salt

⅔ cup butter, chilled

2 Tbsp. fresh lemon juice, *divided*

3½ cups fresh *or* thawed and
drained frozen blueberries

⅔ cup sugar

4 tsp. cornstarch

1 Tbsp. finely grated lemon zest

2 tsp. minced fresh ginger root

1. In a mixing bowl, stir together both flours, brown sugar, and salt.

2. Cut in cold butter with 2 knives or a pastry blender.

3. Remove 1 cup of crumbs and set aside for topping. To remainder in the bowl, add 1 Tbsp. lemon juice.

4. Press lemon crumb mixture into slow cooker to make a tart crust that comes 1″ up the sides.

5. Separately, stir together blueberries, sugar, cornstarch, remaining 1 Tbsp. lemon juice, lemon zest, and ginger.

6. Pour filling into tart crust. Sprinkle with reserved 1 cup crumbs.

7. Cover slow cooker, venting lid at one end with wooden spoon handle or chopstick.

8. Cook on High for 1½–2 hours, until blueberry filling is thickened and bubbling at edges.

9. Remove crock from electrical unit and uncover. Allow to cool for 30–60 minutes before slicing and serving.

TIP

This is a wonderful combination of flavors. Be warned, however, that the slices will be gooey and tender, so don't expect perfect presentation. But the flavor will win you over!

Rhubarb Custard Pie

Makes 8 servings

Prep. Time: 30 minutes ❦ Cooking Time: 1½–2 hours ❦ Standing Time: 30–60 minutes
Ideal slow-cooker size: 6-quart

pastry for a 9" pie
2 eggs
1 cup sugar
pinch salt
¼ tsp. ground nutmeg
2 Tbsp. flour
⅔ cup heavy cream
2½ cups diced rhubarb

1. Take rolled out pastry and fit it into slow cooker as you would line a pie plate, bringing it up the sides 1–2" and gently pushing it into the bottom.

2. In a mixing bowl, whisk eggs until they no longer cling to the whisk.

3. Add sugar, salt, nutmeg, flour, and cream. Whisk again until no lumps remain.

4. Place rhubarb in crust.

5. Pour egg mixture over rhubarb.

6. Cover and cook on High for 1½–2 hours or until knife blade inserted in center comes out clean.

7. Uncover slow cooker and remove crock from electrical unit. Set aside for 30–60 minutes before slicing and serving pie, or allow to cool to room temperature for a totally firm pie.

Why I like this recipe—
This is my favorite rhubarb pie, so simple and so delectable.

Lemon Sponge Pie

Makes 8 servings

Prep. Time: 25 minutes ❧ *Cooking Time: 1½–2½ hours* ❧ *Standing Time: 1–2 hours*
Ideal slow-cooker size: 6-quart

pastry for a 9" pie

3 eggs, separated

¼ tsp. cream of tartar

2 Tbsp. butter

1 cup sugar

finely grated zest of 2 lemons

juice of 2 lemons

3 Tbsp. all-purpose flour

½ tsp. salt

1⅓ cups milk

1. Take rolled out pastry and fit it into slow cooker as you would line a pie plate, bringing it up the sides 1–2" and gently pushing it into the bottom.

2. Beat egg whites and cream of tartar with an electric mixer until they stand up in stiff peaks. Set aside.

3. In a mixing bowl, cream butter, sugar, and egg yolks.

4. Add lemon zest, lemon juice, flour, salt, and milk. Beat again.

5. Fold in beaten egg whites.

6. Pour mixture in pastry-lined slow cooker.

7. Cover and cook on High for 1½–2½ hours, until middle is set and lightly browned.

8. Remove crock from electrical unit and uncover. Allow to cool for 1–2 hours before slicing and serving.

Why I like this recipe—

This is Merle's favorite pie, and it might become yours, too! It's much easier to make than a classic lemon meringue pie, but you get the fluffy top and the wonderful gooey lemon part.

Quiches

Chicken and Spinach Quiche

Makes 6 servings

Prep. Time: 20 minutes ❧ *Cooking Time: 1½–2 hours* ❧ *Standing Time: 20–30 minutes*
Ideal slow-cooker size: 5-quart

pastry for 9" pie

1 cup chopped, cooked chicken

1 cup shredded Swiss cheese

½ cup cooked, chopped spinach, drained (about ⅓ of a 10-oz. frozen pkg., thawed)

¼ cup chopped onion

2 eggs

¾ cup mayonnaise

¾ cup milk

⅛ tsp. pepper

1. Take rolled out pastry and fit it into slow cooker crock as you would line a pie plate, bringing it up the sides 1–2" and gently pushing it into the bottom.

2. In a good-sized bowl, mix together chicken, cheese, spinach, and onion.

3. Spoon into crust.

4. In same bowl, stir together eggs, mayonnaise, milk, and pepper until smooth.

5. Pour over chicken-spinach mixture.

6. Cover. Bake on High 1½–2 hours, or until knife inserted into center of quiche comes out clean.

7. Uncover quickly, swooping lid away from yourself so no water drips on quiche from the inside of the lid. Remove crock from cooker and place on baking rack to cool.

8. Let stand 20–30 minutes, or until firm, before slicing to serve.

Creamy Garden Quiche

Makes 8 servings

Prep. Time: 20 minutes ❦ *Cooking Time: 1½–2 hours* ❦ *Chilling Time: 20 minutes*
Ideal slow-cooker size: 5-quart

pastry for 10" pie

1 lb. feta cheese, crumbled

1½ cups plain yogurt

3 eggs

1 lb. zucchini grated (no need to peel)

4 cloves garlic, minced

4-oz. can green chilies, drained

2–4 Tbsp. minced fresh dill, *or* 2–3 tsp. dried dill

2–4 Tbsp. minced fresh parsley, *or* 2–3 tsp. dried parsley

2–4 Tbsp. minced fresh mint, *or* 2–3 tsp. dried mint

½ cup chopped pine nuts

salt and pepper to taste

1. Take rolled out pastry and fit it into slow cooker crock as you would line a pie plate, bringing it up the sides 1–2" and gently pushing it into the bottom.

2. Combine feta, yogurt, and eggs in a food processor or blender. Process until well blended.

3. In a mixing bowl, combine zucchini, garlic, chilies, dill, parsley, mint, pine nuts, salt, and pepper.

4. Pour creamy mixture into vegetables and herbs. Stir together.

5. Pour into pie crust in crock.

6. Cover. Bake on High 1½–2 hours, or until knife inserted into center of quiche comes out clean.

7. Uncover and remove crock from cooker. Place on baking rack for at least 20 minutes before slicing and serving.

TIP

For a different look, use your mandolin to slice the unpeeled zucchini. And if you've got both green and yellow summer squash, you'll have a beautiful mixture of colorful rounds.

Add-What-You-Like Quiche

Makes 6–8 servings

Prep. Time: 15–20 minutes ❦ Cooking Time 1½–2 hours ❦ Standing Time: 20–30 minutes

Ideal slow-cooker size: 5-quart

pastry for 9" *or* 10" pie

2 cups (½ lb.) grated Swiss cheese

½ cup milk

½ cup mayonnaise

2 Tbsp. flour

¼ cup minced onions

2 eggs

Choose 1 *optional* ingredient listed below:

4 oz. crabmeat

4 oz. fully cooked ham, cubed

6 strips bacon, cooked and crumbled

1½–2 cups chopped fresh spinach

1. Take rolled out pastry and fit it into slow cooker as you would line a pie plate, bringing it up the sides 1–2" and gently pushing it into the bottom.

2. Combine cheese, milk, mayonnaise, flour, onions, eggs, and your choice of one of the optional ingredients in a good-sized bowl.

3. Pour into pie crust.

4. Cover. Bake on High 1½–2 hours, or until knife inserted into center of quiche comes out clean.

5. Quickly remove lid by swooping it away from yourself to prevent water from inside of lid dripping onto quiche. Remove crock from cooker and place on baking rack to cool.

6. Let stand 20–30 minutes, or until firm, before slicing to serve.

Why I like this recipe—

This is about as accommodating a recipe as you can ask for. It takes care of those little bits of good food that somehow just don't get eaten. If you don't have enough of one, you can always combine a couple. And even though browned ground beef or cooked and shredded chicken didn't make it onto the list, they're great here, too.

Mediterranean Quiche

Makes 6–8 servings

Prep. Time: 30 minutes ❧ *Cooking Time: 1½–2 hours* ❧ *Chilling Time: 20–30 minutes*

Ideal slow-cooker size: 5-quart

pastry to make a 9" pie

2–3 Tbsp. oil

¼ cup chopped onion

½ a small eggplant, unpeeled and cubed into ½" pieces (about 2 cups)

2 medium tomatoes, seeded and diced

2 Tbsp. chopped fresh parsley

¼ tsp. dried basil *or* ¾ tsp. chopped fresh basil

½ cup cream *or* evaporated milk

3 eggs

3 Tbsp. grated Parmesan cheese

¼ tsp. minced garlic

¾ tsp. salt

1. Take rolled out pastry and fit it into slow cooker crock as you would line a pie plate, bringing it up the sides 1–2" and gently pushing it into the bottom.

2. Heat oil in skillet over medium heat. Add onion and eggplant cubes and cook gently, just enough to cook off liquid from the eggplant. (This is to keep your quiche from getting watery.)

3. Add tomatoes and cook a few minutes longer, this time to cook off liquid from tomatoes. Using a slotted spoon, lift mixture out of skillet and into crust in crock.

4. In a bowl, whisk together chopped parsley and basil, cream, eggs, cheese, minced garlic, and salt until well blended.

5. Pour over vegetable mixture in crock.

6. Cover. Bake on High 1½–2 hours, or until a knife inserted into center of quiche comes out clean.

7. Uncover quickly so no water drips from lid onto quiche. Remove crock and place on baking rack to cool.

8. Allow to stand 20–30 minutes, or until quiche firms up in center and can be sliced easily.

TIP

I always have a couple of cans of evaporated milk in my cupboard. Evaporated milk is such a great stand-in for cream, which I seldom have in my fridge. And I usually use the low-fat variety, which does just fine here, especially because the eggs and cheese help bring creaminess.

Santa Fe Quiche

Makes 6–8 servings

Prep. Time: 15–20 minutes ❧ *Cooking Time: 1½–2 hours* ❧ *Standing Time: 20–30 minutes*
Ideal slow-cooker size: 5-quart

pastry for 9" pie crust

3 cups grated Mexican cheese

4 eggs

½ cup milk

4-oz. can chopped green chilies, drained

1½ cups chopped fresh tomatoes, deseeded

1. Take rolled out pastry and fit it into slow cooker crock as you would line a pie plate, bringing it up the sides 1–2" and gently pushing it into the bottom.

2. Spread cheese over bottom of pie crust.

3. In a medium-sized bowl, beat eggs and milk together.

4. Stir in drained chilies and chopped tomatoes.

5. Pour into pie crust.

6. Cover. Bake on High 1½–2 hours, or until knife inserted into center of quiche comes out clean.

7. Uncover swiftly by swooping lid away from yourself to prevent water from inside of lid dripping onto quiche. Remove crock from cooker and place on baking rack to cool.

8. Let stand 20–30 minutes, or until firm, before slicing and serving.

TIP

It's worth the time to de-seed the tomatoes. It helps keep the quiche from getting watery, too.

Amish Corn Pie

Makes 6–8 servings

Prep. Time: 30 minutes ❦ *Cooking Time: 1½–2 hours* ❦ *Standing Time: 20 minutes*
Ideal slow-cooker size: 5-quart

pastry for a double-crust 9" pie

3 cups fresh *or* frozen corn

2 Tbsp. chopped onion, optional

1½ cups diced potatoes,
steamed *or* microwaved until just
tender

3 hard-boiled eggs, diced

salt and pepper to taste

2 Tbsp. flour

milk

Why I like this recipe—

This is a traditional meal for those households that grow lots of sweet corn. It is so basic but so absolutely tasty and satisfying. I often make it mid-sweet corn season when we've had lots and know there's lots more to come.

1. Take bottom part of rolled out pastry and fit it into slow cooker crock as you would line a pie plate, bringing it up the sides 1–2" and gently pushing it into the bottom. (Reserve top part of pastry for later.)

2. Combine corn, onions if you wish, potatoes, and eggs in a good sized bowl. Pour into crust in crock.

3. Sprinkle with salt, pepper, and 2 Tbsp. flour.

4. Slowly pour in milk, just enough to barely cover the vegetables.

5. Fit top pastry over filling. Cut several slits (or interesting shapes!) into top crust to allow steam to escape.

6. Cover with lid of cooker. Bake on High 1 hour.

7. Remove cover with a quick swoop (you don't want water to drip on the crust) to allow top crust to dry out and bake through. Continue baking 30–60 minutes, or until milk bubbles around the edges and top crust is dry.

8. Remove crock from cooker and place on wire baking rack to cool.

9. Allow to stand 20 minutes. Then slice and serve.

Spinach and Tomato Quiche

Makes 6 servings

Prep. Time: 20–30 minutes ❧ *Cooking Time: 1½–2 hours* ❧ *Standing Time: 30 minutes*
Ideal slow-cooker size: 5-quart

pastry for 9" pie

2 Tbsp. (¼ stick) butter

½ cup chopped onions

1 tsp. minced garlic

10-oz. pkg. frozen chopped spinach, thawed

1–1½ cups (about 6 oz.) grated Swiss cheese

3 eggs

¾ cup skim milk

½ tsp. salt

1 tsp. dried basil

3 plum tomatoes

1 Tbsp. breadcrumbs

1 Tbsp. Parmesan cheese

1. Take rolled out pastry and fit it into slow cooker crock as you would line a pie plate, bringing it up the sides 1–2" and gently pushing it into the bottom.

2. Melt butter in skillet. Stir in chopped onions and minced garlic. Sauté until veggies just begin to soften.

3. Either squeeze the moisture out of the thawed spinach, or add it to the skillet and cook gently, stirring frequently, until water has evaporated.

4. Stir together spinach and sautéed veggies, grated cheese, eggs, milk, salt, and basil. Pour into pie crust.

5. Slice tomatoes and lay slices over top of filling.

6. Cover cooker. Bake on High 1 hour.

7. Meanwhile, mix together bread crumbs and Parmesan cheese. At end of first hour of baking, sprinkle quiche with crumb-Parmesan cheese mixture.

8. Return cover to cooker and continue baking another 30–60 minutes, or until a knife stuck into the center of the quiche comes out clean.

9. Swoop cover quickly off cooker so condensation on inside of lid doesn't drip on the quiche. Remove crock from cooker and set on baking rack to cool.

10. Let stand 30 minutes, so quiche can firm up but is still warm. Then slice and serve.

Why I like this recipe—

When our one daughter was in college, she lived in a house with a bunch of friends. One of the women made this quiche when it was her turn to cook, and our daughter brought the recipe home because she liked it so much.

A great variation—

When fresh spinach is in season, you can use it instead of frozen spinach. You'll need about 1½ lbs. fresh spinach to start with. Wash it (leaving some of the water droplets on it for steaming later), chop it, and then put it in a good-sized kettle over medium heat and cover it. Cook gently for a few minutes, and it will cook down to about 1½ cups, or roughly 9–10 oz. When it's cooled, squeeze out any excess water before adding to the quiche mixture.

Mushrooms, Tomatoes, and Onion Pie

Makes 6–8 servings

Prep. Time: 15–20 minutes ❦ Cooking Time: 1½–2 hours ❦ Standing Time: 20–30 minutes
Ideal slow-cooker size: 5-quart

pastry for 10" pie

4 spring onions, sliced thin

½ cup halved and de-seeded grape tomatoes

½ cup sliced fresh mushrooms

1 Tbsp. olive oil

6-oz. container plain, non-fat Greek yogurt

1⅓ cups egg substitute

1⅓ cups skim milk

salt and pepper to taste

½ cup shredded low-fat cheddar *or* Colby Jack cheese

1. Take rolled out pastry and fit it into slow cooker crock as you would line a pie plate, bringing it up the sides 1–2" and gently pushing it into the bottom.

2. Sauté onions, tomatoes, and mushrooms in olive oil in skillet for 5 minutes. Drain on paper towel.

3. In a mixing bowl, whisk together yogurt, egg substitute, milk, salt, and pepper.

4. Scatter drained onions, tomatoes, and mushrooms over bottom of pie crust.

5. Sprinkle cheese on top of veggie layer.

6. Pour egg mixture over top.

7. Cover. Bake on High 1½–2 hours, or until knife inserted into center of pie comes out clean.

8. Uncover swiftly, swooping the lid away from yourself, making sure that no water drips from the inside of the lid onto the pie. Remove crock from cooker and place on baking rack to cool.

9. Allow to stand 20–30 minutes to firm up, before slicing to serve.

Why I like this recipe—
This lets the fresh veggies sing. And don't miss how light it is, despite its creaminess.

Fresh Tomato Basil Pie

Makes 6 servings
Prep. Time: 30 minutes ☙ Cooking Time: 1½–2 hours
Ideal slow-cooker size: 5-quart

pastry for 9" pie

1½ cups shredded mozzarella cheese, *divided*

5 plum *or* 4 medium-sized tomatoes

1 cup loosely packed fresh basil leaves, plus additional leaves for garnish

4 cloves garlic

½ cup mayonnaise

¼ cup grated Parmesan cheese

⅛ tsp. ground white pepper

1. Take rolled out pastry and fit it into slow cooker crock as you would line a pie plate, bringing it up the sides 1–2" and gently pushing it into the bottom.

2. Sprinkle ½ cup mozzarella cheese over bottom of pie crust.

3. Cut tomatoes into wedges. Drain in single layer on paper towels for 10 minutes.

4. Arrange tomato wedges on top of cheese in crust.

5. In a food processor, combine basil and garlic, processing until coarsely chopped. Sprinkle over tomatoes.

6. In a medium-sized bowl, combine remaining mozzarella, mayonnaise, Parmesan cheese, and pepper.

7. Spoon cheese mixture over basil mixture, spreading to cover evenly.

8. Cover. Bake on High 1½–2 hours, or until knife inserted into center of pie comes out clean.

9. Uncover quickly, swooping lid away from yourself so no water from inside of lid drips on the pie. Remove crock from cooker and place on baking rack to cool.

10. Let stand 20–30 minutes, or until firm, before slicing to serve.

11. Garnish individual servings with fresh basil leaves.

Tomato Galette

Makes 2 full-size or 6 appetizer-size servings
Prep. Time: 15–20 minutes ❧ Cooking Time: 1½–2 hours
Ideal slow-cooker size: round 5- or 6-quart

9" refrigerated pie crust, or a frozen one, *or* your favorite from-scratch one

½ cup ricotta cheese

¼ cup goat cheese, cubed *or* crumbled

2 tsp. pesto, your choice of flavors

¼ lb. sliced tomatoes

1 egg, slightly beaten

1. Grease interior of round slow cooker crock.

2. Roll out pie dough on a lightly floured surface.

3. In a small bowl, mix ricotta and goat cheeses together.

4. Spread over crust, leaving a 1½" border.

5. Spread pesto over cheeses.

6. Arrange tomato slices on top.

7. Fold edges of crust over filling, pleating as needed, and leaving center uncovered.

8. Brush egg over crust.

9. Using a wide spatula, lift galette up and into crock.

10. Cover. Bake on High for 1½–2 hours, or until pie crust browns well and firms up.

11. Uncover, swooping lid quickly away from yourself to prevent condensation from inside of lid dripping on the galette.

12. Allow to stand for 15 minutes. Then cut into wedges and serve.

TIP

Since this is so attractive before it's cut, get someone to help you lift it out of the cooker uncut— each of you armed with a broad and sturdy metal spatula. Have a platter ready and gently lay it down together! In case you're wondering, lots of kids like this dish!

Mushroom Quiche

Makes 6–8 servings

Prep. Time: 20 minutes ❧ *Cooking Time: 1½–2 hours* ❧ *Standing Time: 20–30 minutes*
Ideal slow-cooker size: 5-quart

pastry for 9" *or* 10" pie

4 Tbsp. (½ stick) butter

1 onion, chopped

½ lb. fresh mushrooms, sliced

1 Tbsp. fresh parsley, chopped

dash of salt

freshly ground black pepper

3 eggs

½ cup light cream

1 cup grated cheddar cheese

1. Take rolled out pastry and fit it into slow cooker crock as you would line a pie plate, bringing it up the sides 1–2" and gently pushing it into the bottom.

2. In a large skillet, sauté onions and mushrooms gently in butter for 5 minutes.

3. Remove skillet from heat and drain off cooking liquid.

4. Stir parsley, salt, and pepper into sautéed veggies.

5. In large mixing bowl, beat together eggs and cream.

6. Stir mushroom mixture into eggs and cream. Fold in cheese.

7. Pour into pie crust.

8. Cover. Bake on High 1½–2 hours, or until knife inserted into center of crust comes out clean.

9. Uncover quickly, swooping lid away from yourself to prevent water from inside of lid from dripping on quiche. Remove crock from cooker and place on baking rack to cool.

10. Let stand 20–30 minutes, or until firm in the center, before slicing and serving.

Why I like this recipe—

Remember the vegetarians in your life, but also those who can't get enough mushrooms.

Artichoke Parmesan Quiche

Makes 6–8 servings

Prep. Time: 15–20 minutes ❦ *Cooking Time: 1½–2 hours* ❦ *Standing Time: 20–30 hours*
Ideal slow-cooker size: 5- or 6-quart

pastry for 9" pie

½ cup grated Parmesan cheese,
plus more for garnish

14-oz. can artichoke hearts,
drained and chopped

1¼ cups shredded Swiss cheese

3-oz. pkg. cream cheese, softened

½ tsp. nutmeg

⅛ tsp. salt

1 cup + 2 Tbsp. evaporated milk

3 eggs

Why I like this recipe—

Okay—a confession. I'm not a big artichoke fan, but so many people are, that I wanted to offer another way to use them. This is so creamy and cheesy, that the artichokes settle into the mix and the quiche is a wonderful combination of flavors and textures. I cut the chokes fairly small, but if you're cooking for artichoke lovers, keep the pieces big enough so that they know what they're biting into.

1. Take rolled out pastry and fit it into slow cooker as you would line a pie plate, bringing it up the sides 1–2" and gently pushing it into the bottom.

2. Sprinkle ½ cup Parmesan cheese over pie crust.

3. Gently squeeze liquid from artichokes, blot them dry and chop fine.

4. Scatter artichokes over Parmesan cheese.

5. Scatter Swiss cheese over artichokes.

6. In small bowl, beat together cream cheese, nutmeg, and salt.

7. Gradually beat milk and one egg at a time into creamed mixture. Beat well after adding each egg until frothy.

8. Pour over quiche filling.

9. Cover. Bake on High 1½–2 hours, or until knife inserted into center of quiche comes out clean.

10. Uncover quickly, swooping lid away from yourself so no water from the inside of the lid drips on the quiche. Remove crock from cooker and place on baking rack to cool.

11. Let stand 20–30 minutes, or until quiche firms up, before slicing to serve.

12. Sprinkle liberally with Parmesan cheese before serving.

Broccoli Quiche

Makes 6–8 servings

Prep. Time: 20–30 minutes ❧ Cooking Time: 1½–2 hours ❧ Standing Time: 20–30 minutes
Ideal slow-cooker size: 5-quart

pastry for 9" pie

3 eggs

⅔ cup chicken *or* vegetable broth

½ cup heavy cream *or* evaporated milk

½ tsp. salt

¼ tsp. Tabasco

¼ cup grated Parmesan cheese, *divided*

2 cups chopped fresh broccoli, *divided*

1 cup grated Swiss cheese, *divided*

¼ cup sliced scallions, *divided*

Some great variations—

I almost never have heavy cream in the house, but I keep a stock of evaporated milk in the pantry. And I almost always have frozen broccoli in the freezer, which I mic until it's thawed when I want to make this deeply satisfying supper. Really, this quiche fits so many occasions— brunch, supper, or dinner. Pair it with a fresh-veggie salad and good bread.

1. Take rolled out pastry and fit it into slow cooker crock as you would line a pie plate, bringing it up the sides 1–2" and gently pushing it into the bottom.

2. Beat eggs with broth, cream, salt, and Tabasco in a bowl. When well mixed, set aside.

3. Sprinkle half the Parmesan cheese over pie crust.

4. Sprinkle half the chopped broccoli over the Parmesan cheese.

5. Sprinkle half the Swiss cheese over the broccoli.

6. Sprinkle half the sliced scallions over the Swiss cheese.

7. Repeat layers of broccoli, Swiss cheese, and scallions.

8. Pour egg mixture over all.

9. Sprinkle with remaining Parmesan cheese.

10. Cover. Bake on High 1½–2 hours, or until knife inserted into center of quiche comes out clean.

11. Uncover swiftly, swooping lid away from yourself to prevent condensation from inside of lid dripping on quiche. Remove crock from cooker and place on baking rack to cool.

12. Let stand 20–30 minutes so quiche can firm up, before slicing and serving.

Asparagus Quiche

Makes 4–6 servings

Prep. Time: 20 minutes ❦ *Cooking Time: 1½–2 hours* ❦ *Standing Time: 20–30 minutes*
Ideal slow-cooker size: 5-quart

pastry for a 9" pie

3 cups fresh asparagus, cut in small pieces

2 cups shredded sharp cheddar cheese

1 cup mayonnaise

2 tsp. lemon juice

1. Take rolled out pastry and fit it into slow cooker crock as you would line a pie plate, bringing it up the sides 1–2" and gently pushing it into the bottom.

2. In a mixing bowl, gently combine asparagus, cheese, mayonnaise, and lemon juice.

3. Spoon into pie crust.

4. Cover. Bake on High 1½–2 hours, or until quiche is firm in center.

5. Swoop lid off quickly so no water from the inside of the lid drips on the quiche.

6. Remove crock from cooker and place on wire baking rack to cool.

7. Allow to stand 20–30 minutes, or until firm enough to slice.

TIP

Because you don't cook the asparagus ahead of putting into the crock, it retains its fresh and distinctive flavor. If you want the asparagus to stand front and center, use a milder cheddar so it doesn't compete flavor-wise.

Breakfast Torte

Makes 8 servings
Prep. Time: 20 minutes ❦ *Cooking Time: 3–4 hours*
Ideal slow-cooker size: 4-quart

2 8-oz. pkgs. refrigerated crescent rolls

4 eggs

1 lb. cooked, crumbled sausage

¾ cup shredded mozzarella

¼ cup crumbled feta

2 green onions, chopped

¾ cup halved grape tomatoes

½ tsp. dried basil

1. Take 1 package of dough and press it into bottom of greased slow cooker.

2. Sprinkle with sausage, mozzarella, green onions, tomatoes, and then feta. Do not mix.

3. In a bowl, beat eggs and basil together.

4. Pour evenly over layers in slow cooker.

5. Take remaining package of dough and flatten it into the shape of the slow cooker. Lay it on top of torte to make a final layer.

6. Cover and cook on High for 3–4 hours until dough is puffy and eggs are set.

TIP
Vary the veggies and meat according to what your family likes and what you have on hand.

Yeast Breads

Daily Bread

Makes one 9" loaf

Prep. Time: 30 minutes ❦ *Cooking Time: 2–3 hours*
Rising Time: 1 hour ❦ *Ideal slow-cooker size: 6-quart*

1½ cups whole wheat flour, *divided*

2 tsp. instant yeast

1 tsp. salt

3 Tbsp. honey

1 Tbsp. oil, plus a little more for the bowl

¾ cup warm water

1½ cups unbleached all-purpose flour

1. In mixing bowl, combine 1 cup whole wheat flour, yeast, salt, honey, oil, and warm water. Beat well for 1 minute.

2. Stir in remaining ½ cup whole wheat flour and gradually add the all-purpose flour until a thick dough is forming.

3. Knead by hand for 5 minutes.

4. Pour a little oil over the dough and bowl, turning ball of dough to grease all sides. Cover with damp kitchen towel and set in warm place to rise until doubled, about 1 hour.

5. On counter or board, press dough flat with hands or rolling pin. Roll up into loaf, tucking ends under and pinching bottom seam securely.

6. Place loaf in greased loaf pan, seam-side down. Set pan on metal trivet or jar ring in slow cooker.

7. Cover and cook on High for 2–3 hours, or until top is firm, bread is pulling away from the sides of the pan, and an instant-read thermometer inserted in middle of loaf registers 200°.

8. Wearing oven gloves to protect your knuckles, remove pan from cooker. Turn loaf out onto wire rack and allow to cool before slicing.

A great variation—

This is a basic whole wheat bread with excellent flavor. You can increase the amount of whole wheat flour and decrease the white flour, but consider adding 1–2 tsp. vital wheat gluten to keep the bread light and willing to rise.

Crockery Oatmeal Bread

Makes one 9" loaf

Prep. Time: 30 minutes ❦ Cooking Time: 2–3 hours ❦ Standing Time: 30 minutes
Rising Time: 1 hour ❦ Ideal slow-cooker size: 6-quart

½ cup rolled oats

1¼ cups whole wheat flour, *divided*

¼ cup brown sugar

1½ tsp. salt

1 Tbsp. butter

1 cup boiling water

1½ tsp. instant yeast

1½ cups unbleached all-purpose flour, *divided*

1 Tbsp. oil

Why I like this recipe—

This bread is wonderful toasted for breakfast. It's also one of my favorite gifts to take to new neighbors because fresh homemade bread is such a treat.

1. In a mixing bowl, combine oats, ¼ cup whole wheat flour, brown sugar, salt, butter, and boiling water. Set aside to cool to room temperature, about 30 minutes.

2. Stir yeast into lukewarm mixture. Stir in remaining 1 cup whole wheat flour.

3. Add 1 cup all-purpose flour. Begin to knead, adding remaining ½ cup gradually as needed to make dough. Knead for 5 minutes.

4. Pour oil over dough and bowl, turning dough ball to grease all sides. Cover with damp kitchen towel and set in warm place to rise until doubled, about 1 hour.

5. On counter or board, press dough flat with hands or rolling pin. Roll up into loaf, tucking ends under and pinching bottom seam securely.

6. Place loaf in greased loaf pan. Set pan on metal trivet or jar ring in slow cooker.

7. Cover and cook on High for 2–3 hours, or until top is firm, loaf is pulling away from sides of pan, and instant-read thermometer inserted in middle of loaf registers 200°.

8. Wearing oven gloves to protect your knuckles, remove pan from cooker. Turn loaf out onto wire rack and allow to cool before slicing.

Artisan Bread in the Crock

Makes one 9" loaf

Prep. Time: 30 minutes   ☙   Cooking Time 2–3 hours   ☙   Rising Time: 14–26 hours
Ideal slow-cooker size: 6-quart

2 cups whole wheat flour

2 cups unbleached all-purpose flour

1¼ tsp. salt

¼ tsp. instant yeast

2 cups warm water, *divided*

3 Tbsp. coarse cornmeal, *divided*

1. In a large bowl with a tight-fitting lid (or use plastic wrap) mix flours, salt, and yeast.

2. Add 1½ cups water. Mix. Add more water gradually, up to 2 cups, until a wet dough is formed, like very thick mud.

3. Cover tightly and set in a dark place at room temperature for at least 12 hours and not more than 24 hours.

4. Grease a large square of parchment paper and place in slow cooker. Sprinkle with 2 Tbsp. cornmeal.

5. Pour and prod the dough out of the bowl onto the cornmeal-sprinkled parchment in the cooker.

6. Sprinkle with remaining 1 Tbsp. cornmeal.

7. Cover and allow to rest for 2–3 hours.

8. Turn slow cooker on to High and bake for 2–3 hours, until top is firm and instant-read thermometer inserted in middle of loaf registers 200°.

9. Wearing oven gloves to protect your knuckles, lift parchment with loaf out of slow cooker. Set on wire rack to cool before slicing.

TIP

The long rise replaces the kneading and the small pinch of yeast gives the loaf a less yeasty taste, that "artisan" flavor and holes that I love. Using the slow cooker means that the loaf will be a bit flatter than one baked in a traditional oven, but I am totally willing to trade that for the convenience.

Some great variations—

You can experiment with adding olives, dried tomatoes, or herbs before placing in the slow cooker.

Dark Rye Bread

Makes one 9" loaf

Prep. Time: 30 minutes ❧ *Cooking Time: 2–3 hours*
Rising Time: 1 hour ❧ *Ideal slow-cooker size: 6-quart*

1 Tbsp. instant yeast

2 Tbsp. unsweetened cocoa powder

1 tsp. caraway seeds

2 Tbsp. blackstrap molasses

1 Tbsp. sugar

½ tsp. salt

1 Tbsp. oil, plus more for bowl

1 cup water

2 cups all-purpose unbleached flour, + 1 Tbsp., *optional*, for sprinkling

1½ cups whole-grain rye flour

1. In mixing bowl, combine yeast, cocoa powder, caraway seeds, molasses, sugar, salt, oil, water, and all-purpose flour. Beat for 1 minute.

2. Add rye flour gradually, first stirring and then using hands to make a stiff dough.

3. Knead for 5 minutes.

4. Pour oil over dough and bowl, turning dough ball to grease all sides. Cover with damp kitchen towel and set in warm place to rise until doubled, about 1 hour.

5. On counter or board, press dough flat with hands. Roll up into a loaf. Tuck edges under to form a round or oblong loaf.

6. Place loaf in center of large square of parchment paper and gently lift it into the slow cooker.

7. With a sharp knife, slash an X in the loaf about ½" deep. Sprinkle with 1 Tbsp. flour if you wish.

8. Cover and cook on High for 2–3 hours, until top is firm and instant-read thermometer inserted in middle of loaf registers 200°. The X will have dramatically opened up to make a rustic-looking loaf.

9. Wearing oven gloves to protect your knuckles, remove paper with loaf from cooker. Set on wire rack and allow to cool before slicing.

Why I like this recipe—

Dark rye bread makes excellent grilled reuben sandwiches. It also is nice as part of Sunday supper like I remember from a visit to Germany: a platter of sliced meat and cheese, some pickles, and bread for making open-faced sandwiches.

English Muffin Loaf

Makes one 9" loaf

Prep. Time: 20 minutes ❦ Cooking Time: 2–3 hours
Rising Time: 1 hour ❦ Ideal slow-cooker size: 6-quart

2½ cups unbleached all-purpose
flour, *divided*

1 Tbsp. instant yeast

1 Tbsp. sugar

1 tsp. salt

¼ tsp. baking soda

1 cup warm milk

1 Tbsp. coarse cornmeal

1. In a mixing bowl, combine 1 cup flour, yeast, sugar, salt, baking soda, and warm milk.

2. Beat with electric mixer for 3 minutes, scraping bowl occasionally.

3. Stir in remaining 1½ cups flour to make a stiff batter.

4. Grease loaf pan. Sprinkle with cornmeal.

5. Pour batter in prepared pan. Cover with kitchen towel and set aside for 1 hour to rise.

6. Place risen loaf on metal trivet or jar ring in slow cooker.

7. Cover and cook on High for 2–3 hours, until loaf is firm on top and instant-read thermometer inserted in middle of loaf registers 200°.

8. Wearing oven gloves to protect your knuckles, remove pan from cooker. Turn loaf out onto wire rack and allow to cool before slicing.

Why I like this recipe—
    This is a great starting recipe for beginning bread bakers because the mixer does the kneading. I treat slices of this bread just like store-bought English muffins.

Tomato Herb Bread

Makes one 9" loaf

Prep. Time: 30 minutes ❦ Cooking Time: 2–3 hours
Rising Time: 1 hour ❦ Ideal slow-cooker size: 6-quart

¾ cup peeled, chopped tomatoes (canned are fine)

I tsp. dried dill weed

½ tsp. dried basil

¼ tsp. dried oregano

I tsp. salt

I Tbsp. honey

I Tbsp. melted butter

2 tsp. instant yeast

2½ cups unbleached all-purpose flour

a little oil for the bowl

1. In food processor or blender, puree tomatoes, dill, basil, oregano, salt, honey, and 1 Tbsp. butter.

2. Pour mixture into mixing bowl. Add yeast. Stir.

3. Gradually add flour, stirring and then kneading by hand to form a smooth dough.

4. Knead for 5 minutes. Pour a little oil on dough and bowl, turning ball of dough to grease all sides.

5. Cover with a damp kitchen towel and set aside in a warm spot to rise for 1 hour or until doubled.

6. On counter or board, press dough flat with hands or rolling pin. Roll up into loaf, tucking ends under and pinching bottom seam securely.

7. Place loaf in greased loaf pan. Set pan on metal trivet or jar ring in slow cooker.

8. Cover and cook on High for 2–3 hours, or until top is firm, loaf is pulling away from sides of pan, and instant-read thermometer inserted in middle of loaf registers 200°.

9. Wearing oven gloves to protect your knuckles, remove pan from cooker. Turn loaf out onto wire rack and allow to cool before slicing.

Why I like this recipe—

This is my hands-down favorite bread to use in grilled cheese sandwiches. One of my friends uses it for tomato, basil, and mozzarella grilled cheese sandwiches in the summer. And this is definitely a summer-friendly recipe since the slow cooker won't heat up the house like the oven would!

Zucchini Sandwich Buns

Makes 12 rolls

Prep. Time: 30 minutes ❦ *Cooking Time: 2–3 hours*
Rising Time: 1 hour ❦ *Ideal slow-cooker size: 6-quart*

1½ cups shredded zucchini

⅓ cup warm water

⅓ cup warm milk

3 Tbsp. oil

2 Tbsp. instant yeast

⅓ cup sugar

2 tsp. salt

1 cup whole wheat flour

3 cups unbleached all-purpose flour, *divided*

1. In a mixing bowl, combine zucchini, water, milk, oil, yeast, sugar, salt, and whole wheat flour. Do not pour off any liquid from zucchini.

2. Add unbleached flour a cup at a time, stirring until soft dough forms.

3. Knead 5 minutes. The dough will be sticky, but persevere!

4. Pour a little oil on dough and bowl, turning dough ball to grease it. Cover with damp kitchen towel and set aside to rise until doubled, about 1 hour.

5. Divide dough into 12 pieces. Press and roll them into balls.

6. Grease a large square of parchment paper and tuck it into the slow cooker.

7. Place rolls inside slow cooker.

8. Cover and cook on High for 1½–3 hours, checking at 1½ hours by gently pulling apart two rolls in the middle and checking to make sure they are not doughy yet.

9. Wearing oven gloves to protect your knuckles, lift parchment with rolls out of cooker. Set it on wire rack to cool.

TIP

Separate rolls and keep tightly covered at room temperature for 2 days, or wrap tightly and freeze. They are excellent for hamburgers, sloppy joes, or sandwiches.

Granny's Potato Rolls

Makes 8 servings

Prep. Time: 30 minutes ❦ *Cooking Time: 1½–2½ hours*
Rising Time: 1½ hours ❦ *Ideal slow-cooker size: 6-quart*

I small potato, to make ½ cup mashed potato

I cup warm milk

4 Tbsp. (½ stick) butter, room temperature

⅓ cup sugar

I cup whole wheat flour

I Tbsp. instant yeast

I tsp. salt

I egg, beaten

3 cups unbleached all-purpose flour, *divided*

1. Peel the potato and dice. Cook in microwave or in saucepan on stove top with 2–3 Tbsp. water until soft. Beat and mash well to make very smooth mashed potato.

2. Combine warm mashed potato with milk, butter, sugar, whole wheat flour, and yeast. Cover with kitchen towel and set aside for 30 minutes.

3. Stir in salt, egg, and 1 cup all-purpose flour. Gradually add up to 2 cups more of unbleached flour, stirring to make soft dough.

4. Knead dough for 3–5 minutes. It will be sticky and soft, but that will make tender rolls, so be patient!

5. Pour a little oil on dough and bowl, turning ball of dough until all sides are greased. Cover with damp kitchen towel and set aside to rise until double, about 1 hour.

6. Divide dough into 8–10 pieces. Shape into balls.

7. Grease a large square of parchment and tuck it into slow cooker. Space rolls evenly on parchment in cooker.

Why I like this recipe—

This recipe is courtesy of my friend, whose grandmother used this dough to make lots of varieties of sweet treats. I just stick with these dinner rolls because they are so good and simple.

8. Cover and cook on High for 1½–2½ hours, checking to see if rolls are done by pulling apart two in the center to make sure they are not doughy yet.

9. Wearing oven gloves to protect your knuckles, remove parchment with rolls from slow cooker. Set on wire rack to cool.

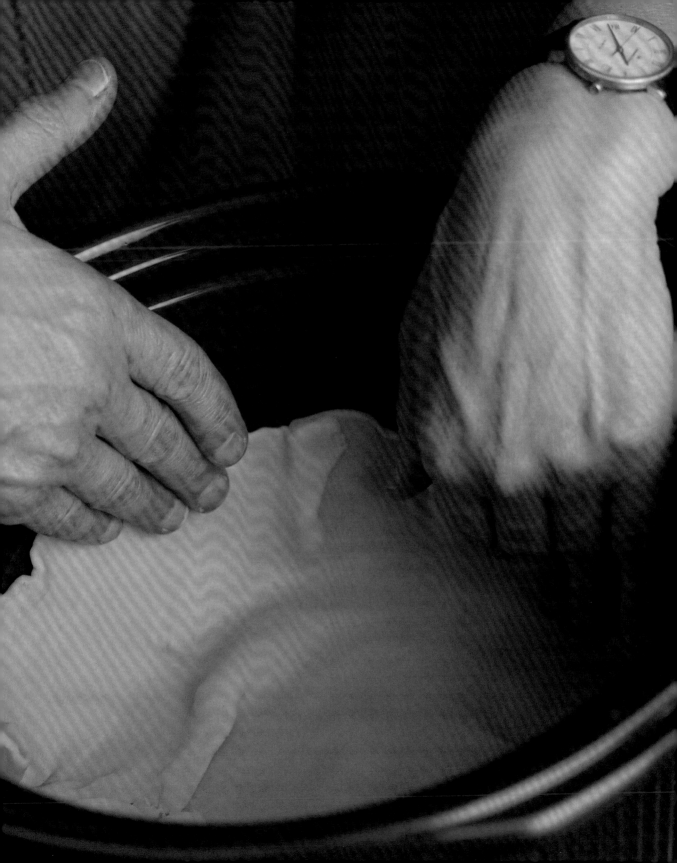

Pizzas

Deep-Dish Pepperoni Pizza

Makes 4 servings
Prep. Time: 30 minutes ❧ Cooking Time: 2½ hours
Rising Time: about 1 hour ❧ Ideal slow-cooker size: 6– quart

½ cup unbleached all-purpose flour

½ cup whole wheat bread flour

½ tsp. instant yeast

½ tsp. salt

2 Tbsp. olive oil, *divided*

⅓ cup warm water

½ cup thick pizza sauce

I cup shredded mozzarella cheese

3 oz. sliced pepperoni, *or to taste*

½ tsp. dried basil

1. In a medium mixing bowl, combine flours, yeast, salt, 1 Tbsp. olive oil, and water. Stir to form a shaggy dough.

2. Knead for several minutes until a stiff dough forms. Knead into a ball.

3. Pour in remaining 1 Tbsp. olive oil and grease the ball and the bowl. Cover with a cloth and set aside in a warm place for approximately 1 hour.

4. After 1 hour, grease slow cooker.

5. Remove ball of dough to counter. Roll out with a rolling pin into a large oval that is larger by a few inches than slow cooker.

6. Lift the dough into the slow cooker and gently pull it and shape it so that the dough lines the crock and comes up 2–3" on the sides.

7. Cook for 1½ hours on High, uncovered. Dough should be firm and getting brown at edges.

8. Spread pizza sauce on the floor of the dough. Sprinkle with cheese. Layer on pepperoni. Sprinkle with basil.

9. Cook an additional hour on High, with lid placed back on cooker and vented with a wooden spoon handle or chopstick at one end. Toppings should be hot through and the cheese melted.

TIP

Use a large spatula to coax the pizza out of the cooker onto a platter, then cut it into slices. Or use a plastic or silicone knife to slice the pizza directly in the slow cooker and lift out the slices one by one.

Artisan Pizza in the Crock

Makes 2–4 servings
Prep. Time: 30 minutse 🌱 Cooking Time: 2½ hours
Rising Time: 6–8 hours 🌱 Ideal slow-cooker size: 6 quart

1 cup unbleached white bread
flour

⅛ tsp. instant yeast

¼ tsp. salt

⅓ cup water

1–2 Tbsp. coarse cornmeal

⅓ cup thick pizza sauce

handful spinach leaves

4 oz. sliced smoked Gouda

2 garlic cloves, chopped

1. In a bowl with a lid, mix flour, yeast, salt, and water. The dough should be shaggy and on the dry side. Cover bowl tightly and set aside in a warm place for 6–8 hours.

2. Lightly grease slow cooker. Sprinkle bottom of slow cooker with cornmeal to help prevent sticking.

3. Take ball of dough in hand and stretch it gently to form a rough oval, slightly larger than the floor of the slow cooker. The dough will be sticky and you can flour it lightly for easier handling.

4. Place stretched dough in crock so that it comes up the sides 1".

5. With the lid off, cook the crust on High for 1½ hours, until crust is firm and browning at edges.

6. Smooth the pizza sauce over the floor of the crust. Spread spinach leaves over the sauce in an even layer, topping with a layer of Gouda slices. Sprinkle with chopped garlic.

7. Place the lid on the cooker with a wooden spoon handle or chopstick venting it at one end.

8. Cook for an hour, until spinach leaves are wilted and cheese is melted.

9. Slip a wide spatula under the pizza and remove it to a cutting board to slice.

TIP

The long rise of this dough takes the place of kneading and the tiny bit of yeast makes it taste more like pizzeria dough. If you misjudged your time, simply pop the covered bowl of dough in the fridge after its long rise. It can keep for up to 3 days—just bring it to room temperature again before trying to stretch it into an oval.

Cheese-Stuffed Pizza

Makes 6 servings
Prep. Time: 30 minutes ❦ Cooking Time: 2 hours ❦ Standing Time: 20 minutes
Ideal slow-cooker size: 5-quart

11- *or* 13-oz. pkg. refrigerated pizza dough

1½ cups shredded mozzarella, *divided*

½ cup thick pizza sauce

1 cup *or* less favorite pizza toppings such as chopped veggies *or* cooked meat

1. Divide dough in half. Roll and/or stretch each piece of dough into an oval to match the size of the bottom of the crock.

2. Place 1 dough oval in greased slow cooker, pushing and stretching it out to the edges. Sprinkle with ½ cup mozzarella.

3. Place the other dough oval on top of the cheese, stretching it to the edges of the crock.

4. Cook, uncovered, for 1 hour on High. Dough should be puffy and getting brown at edges.

5. Spread pizza sauce on top. Sprinkle with remaining 1 cup cheese and any toppings you wish.

6. Place lid on cooker with chopstick or wooden spoon handle venting it at one end.

7. Cook on High for an additional hour, until toppings are heated through.

Why I like this recipe—
Kids are especially fond of this cheesy goodness!

White Pizza in the Crock

Makes 4 servings
Prep. Time: 30 minutes ❦ Cooking Time: 3 hours
Ideal slow-cooker size: 6-quart

½ cup + 1 Tbsp. unbleached all-purpose flour, *divided*

½ cup whole wheat bread flour

½ tsp. instant yeast

½ tsp. salt

2 Tbsp. olive oil, *divided*

⅓ cup warm water

⅔ cup cottage cheese

1 garlic clove

2 Tbsp. grated Parmesan cheese

1 cup loose fresh spinach leaves

2 Tbsp. chopped olives of choice

1 tsp. dried basil

1. In a medium mixing bowl, combine ½ cup all-purpose flour, whole wheat flour, yeast, salt, 1 Tbsp. olive oil, and water. Stir to form a shaggy dough.

2. Knead for several minutes until a stiff dough forms. Knead into a ball.

3. Pour in remaining 1 Tbsp. olive oil and grease the ball and the bowl. Cover with a damp cloth and set aside in a warm place for approximately 1 hour.

4. Make the white sauce. Place cottage cheese, garlic clove, Parmesan, and 1 Tbsp. all-purpose flour in food processor or blender. Process until smooth. Set aside.

5. Place ball of dough on counter. Roll out with a rolling pin into a large oval that is larger by a few inches than slow cooker.

6. Lift the dough into greased slow cooker and gently pull it and shape it so that the dough lines the crock and comes up 2–3" on the sides.

7. Cook for 2 hours on High, uncovered. Dough should be firm and getting brown at edges.

8. Spread spinach leaves evenly over dough. Dollop and spread white sauce over spinach leaves. Sprinkle with chopped olives and basil.

9. Cover cooker with lid and vent lid at one end with a wooden spoon handle or chopstick.

10. Cook an additional hour on High, until spinach is wilted and toppings are heated through.

A great variation—

Slip some sundried tomato slices in with the filling, or top with thinly sliced fresh tomatoes. I love the ease of this white sauce because I don't have to cook anything ahead of time, just whiz it up in a blender or food processor!

Buffalo Chicken Stromboli

Makes 4–6 servings

Prep. Time: 30 minutes ❧ Cooking Time 2–3 hours ❧ Standing Time: 5 hours or overnight

Ideal slow-cooker size: 6-quart

1 ball frozen pizza dough, about 15 oz.

2 cups cooked, shredded chicken

2 green onions, sliced

1 cup shredded mozzarella cheese

⅓ cup shredded sharp cheddar cheese

½ cup ranch dressing

3 Tbsp. Frank's RedHot® Sauce

few drops liquid smoke, *optional*

TIP

If you keep the same proportions (2 cups filling, ½–⅔ cup sauce, 1 ⅓ cups cheese), you can play around with different flavor combinations. Change it up according to what you have on hand and what your family likes.

A great variation—

If you don't have Frank's RedHot® Sauce, use a tablespoon or two of the hot sauce you do have, adding white vinegar and a bit of minced garlic to make up 3 tablespoons.

1. Thaw pizza dough per package directions, usually about 5 hours at room temperature or overnight in the fridge.

2. Grease bottom of slow cooker crock. Turn on High and set aside to preheat while you assemble the stromboli.

3. On a lightly floured surface, roll dough out into rectangle, approximately 8″ x 12″.

4. Sprinkle and spread chicken, onions, and both cheeses evenly over the dough, leaving a 1″ border on all sides.

5. In a small bowl, mix ranch dressing, RedHot® Sauce, and optional liquid smoke.

6. Drizzle evenly over layers on dough.

7. Gently tug one short side of the dough over to meet the other short side, nudging the stromboli onto its side as needed, encasing the filling. Pinch seam well to seal.

8. Ease the stromboli into the middle of a large square of parchment paper with the seam side down.

9. Pick up the parchment like a sling with the stromboli in the middle and place it in the hot slow cooker.

10. Cover and cook on High for 2–3 hours, until dough is firm and browned at edges, and filling is oozy and hot.

11. Lift stromboli out, using parchment as a sling. Slice and serve, or else place stromboli on baking sheet and run it under the broiler for a few minutes (watch closely!) to get brown and bubbly on top.

Crazy-Crust Pizza

Makes 4 servings

Prep. Time: 20 minutes ❧ Cooking Time: 2 hours

Ideal slow-cooker size: 6-quart

1 ⅓ cups all-purpose flour

½ tsp. salt

1 tsp. Italian herb seasoning

2 eggs

⅔ cup milk

½ cup thick pizza sauce

1 cup shredded mozzarella

½ cup favorite pizza toppings

TIP

May substitute whole wheat flour for the all-purpose flour.

1. Grease slow cooker. Turn on High to preheat while you mix up the batter.

2. In a mixing bowl, mix flour, salt, Italian herb seasoning, egg, and milk until smooth.

3. Pour into heated, greased cooker. Put lid on, with one side vented with a wooden spoon handle or chopstick.

4. Cook on High for 1 hour, until crust is set and starting to brown at edges.

5. Spread pizza sauce over crust. Sprinkle with mozzarella and any toppings you wish.

6. Place lid on cooker, venting it again.

7. Cook an additional hour on High, until toppings are heated through.

Some great variations—

I have good success with using odds and ends from my fridge as pizza toppings. Recently, I used about 2 cups broccoli florets and ½ cup chopped red onion. I microwaved them just a bit to take off the raw edge, then I sprinkled them over the pizza sauce with some chopped cilantro and some leftover pork marsala. Then I sprinkled the mozzarella over all. Delicious!

Zucchini Crust Pizza

Makes 6 servings

Prep. Time: 20 minutes ❦ *Cooking Time: 4–5 hours*

Ideal slow-cooker size: 4-quart

2½ cups packed, grated zucchini

2 eggs

⅓ cup all-purpose flour

1 cup shredded mozzarella, *divided*

¼ cup freshly grated Parmesan

¼ tsp. dried basil

¼ tsp. dried marjoram

freshly ground pepper, to taste

½ cup thick pizza sauce

¼ cup chopped green olives

¼ cup chopped mushrooms

2 cloves garlic, chopped

1. In a mixing bowl, combine zucchini, eggs, flour, ½ cup mozzarella, Parmesan, basil, marjoram, and pepper.

2. Pour mixture into greased slow cooker. Smooth top.

3. Cover and cook on Low for 3–4 hours, until set.

4. Smooth pizza sauce on top of baked crust. Add olives, mushrooms, and garlic.

5. With lid off, cook an additional 30–60 minutes on Low until toppings are hot and any moisture has evaporated at sides.

TIP

Vary toppings according to what you like on your pizzas. I love this recipe for using up zucchini in the summer, although it's possible to use frozen shredded zucchini, too.

Polish Pizza

Makes 4 servings

Prep. Time: 30 minutes & Cooking Time: 3 hours

Ideal slow-cooker size: 6-quart

1 Tbsp. butter

3 cups shredded, unpeeled potatoes

½ cup finely diced onion

3 Tbsp. spicy brown mustard

16-oz. bag sauerkraut, drained well

13-oz. ring kielbasa, sliced

¾ cup shredded Swiss cheese

1. Grease crock with butter and turn slow cooker on High to preheat.

2. Place potatoes and onion in a kitchen towel or cloth that can get stained. Squeeze firmly to press out as much liquid as possible from potatoes and onions. Discard liquid.

3. Sprinkle onion and potatoes into cooker. Cover, but vent the lid at one end with a wooden spoon handle or chopstick.

4. Cook on High for 1½ hours. The potatoes and onions should be getting browned at edges.

5. Gently spread mustard over potato crust. Sprinkle with sauerkraut and arrange kielbasa slices on top. Sprinkle cheese over all.

6. Cook on High for another 1½ hours, again with lid vented at one end.

Why I like this recipe—
This is a hearty "pizza" that I like to make on cold, snowy days. It is a meal in itself.

Granolas

New Guinea Granola

Makes 8 servings

Prep. Time: 15 minutes ❧ Cooking Time: 2–3 hours ❧ Chilling Time: 1 hour
Ideal slow-cooker size: 5- or 6-quart

3 cups dry quick oats
3 cups dry rolled oats
½ cup dry oat bran
½ cup milk powder
⅔ cup honey
⅔ cup vegetable oil
1 tsp. vanilla
cinnamon
¾ cup slivered almonds
½ cup sunflower seeds
¾ cup Craisins® *or* raisins

1. Grease interior of slow cooker crock.

2. Mix all ingredients well in crock except cinnamon, almonds, seeds, and Craisins®. Stir up from bottom to make sure everything gets incorporated.

3. Cover, but vent the lid by propping it open with a chopstick or wooden spoon handle. Or if you're using an oval cooker, turn the lid sideways.

4. Cook on High for 1 hour, stirring up from the bottom and around the sides every 20 minutes or so. (Set a timer so you don't forget!)

5. Switch the cooker to Low. Stir in almonds, sunflower seeds and Craisins®. Bake another 1–2 hours, still stirring every 20 minutes or so.

6. Granola is done when it eventually browns a bit and looks dry.

7. Pour granola onto parchment or a large baking sheet to cool and crisp up more.

8. If you like clumps, no need to stir it while it cools. Otherwise, break up the granola with a spoon or your hands as it cools.

9. When completely cooled, store in airtight container.

Why I like this recipe—

Our daughters claim this is among the best granolas they've ever eaten. It's got an interesting history—it came from their aunt, who got it from her sister, who she thinks learned to make it while traveling in Asia. Everyone along the way has adjusted the recipe and made it their own, of course, which you're expected to do, too!

Ellen's Granola

Makes 12 servings

Prep. Time: 20 minutes   ❦   Cooking time: 1½–2½ hours   ❦   Chilling Time: 1–1½ hours

Ideal slow-cooker size: 6- or 7-quart

1 cup vegetable oil

1 cup honey

8 cups dry rolled oats

1 cup wheat germ

1 cup powdered milk

1 cup shredded unsweetened coconut

½ cup soya flour

1 cup sunflower seeds

1 cup chopped nuts, your favorite

¼ cup sesame seeds

1 cup pumpkin seeds

½ tsp. salt

1. Grease interior of slow cooker crock.

2. Combine oil and honey in a microwave-safe bowl. Heat for 1 minute on High. Stir until well blended.

3. Combine all other ingredients in a big bowl. Stir together well.

4. Pour oil/honey mixture over dries, mixing thoroughly. Stir up from bottom to make sure everything gets incorporated.

5. Pour everything into the slow cooker crock.

6. Cover, but vent the lid by propping it open with a chopstick or wooden spoon handle. Or if you're using an oval cooker, turn the lid sideways.

7. Cook on High for 1 hour, stirring up from the bottom and around the sides every 20 minutes or so. (Set a timer so you don't forget!)

8. Switch the cooker to Low. Bake another 1–2 hours, still stirring every 20 minutes or so.

9. Granola is done when it eventually browns a bit and looks dry.

10. Pour granola onto parchment or a large baking sheet to cool and crisp up more.

11. If you like clumps, no need to stir it while it cools. Otherwise, break up the granola with a spoon or your hands as it cools.

12. When completely cooled, store in airtight container.

TIP

Here's how Ellen's husband, Keith, likes to eat Ellen's Granola: 1. Fill a large soup bowl ⅓ full of the granola. 2. Add 2–3 large dollops of yogurt. 3. Scoop on a generous topping of applesauce. 4. Add a little honey if you want it sweeter, or a dash of molasses if you're feeling a bit anemic (iron, you know). 5. Add milk and gently mix until it's the right consistency. 6. Sometimes I skip the milk if I'm in the mood for crunchy granola.

Chocolate Buckwheat Granola

Makes 6–7 servings

Prep. Time: 20–25 minutes ❦ Cooking Time: 2–3 hours ❦ Chilling Time: 1 hour
Ideal slow-cooker size: 5- or 6-quart

3 cups dry rolled oats

½ cup wheat germ, toasted or not

1 cup buckwheat groats (these are uncooked, shelled buckwheat; they look like little triangular nubbins)

1 cup shredded sweetened coconut

1 cup hazelnuts or other unsalted nuts that you have on hand

¼ cup sesame seeds

⅓ cup honey

⅓ cup vegetable oil

½ tsp. salt

¼ cup dark brown sugar

½ cup unsweetened cocoa powder

1 tsp. vanilla

1. Grease interior of slow cooker crock.

2. In a good-sized bowl, stir together rolled oats, wheat germ, buckwheat groats, coconut, hazelnuts, and sesame seeds.

3. In a microwave-safe bowl, or in a small saucepan, warm together honey, oil, salt, brown sugar, cocoa powder, and vanilla. Stir until smooth.

4. Pour wet ingredients over dry, mixing up from the bottom and around the sides until well combined.

5. Pour into slow cooker crock. Cover, but vent the lid by propping it open with a chopstick or wooden spoon handle. Or if you're using an oval cooker, turn the lid sideways.

6. Cook on High for 1 hour, stirring up from the bottom and around the sides every 20 minutes or so. (Set a timer so you don't forget!)

7. Switch the cooker to Low. Bake another 1–2 hours, still stirring every 20 minutes or so. Granola is done when it eventually browns a bit and looks dry.

8. Pour granola onto parchment or a large baking sheet to cool and crisp up more.

9. If you like clumps, no need to stir further it while it cools. Otherwise, continue to break up the granola with a spoon or your hands as it cools.

10. When completely cooled, store in airtight container.

Why I like this recipe—
We like this topped with berries and plain yogurt. Sometimes we sprinkle on some chocolate chips!

Pecan Granola

Makes 6–8 servings

Prep. Time: 20 minutes   Cooking Time: 1½–2 hours   Chilling Time: 1 hour

Ideal slow-cooker size: 5-quart

6 cups dry oats, quick *or* rolled

¾ cup wheat germ

½ cup milk powder

½ cup brown sugar, packed

½ cup unsweetened shredded coconut, *optional*

¼ cup sesame seeds, *optional*

1 cup chopped pecans

½ cup + 2 Tbsp. vegetable oil

½ cup + 2 Tbsp. honey

2 Tbsp. water

1½ tsp. vanilla

1 cup raisins

A great variation—

If you love pecans as much as I do, it doesn't hurt to drop the raisins and double the amount of pecans in this recipe!

1. Grease interior of slow cooker crock.

2. In a good-sized bowl, mix together all dry ingredients—oats, wheat germ, milk powder, brown sugar, coconut, and sesame seeds if you wish, and pecans.

3. In a separate bowl, combine oil, honey, water, and vanilla well.

4. Pour wet ingredients over dry. Stir well, remembering to stir up from the bottom, using either a strong spoon or your clean hands.

5. Pour mixture into crock. Cover, but vent the lid by propping it open with a chopstick or wooden spoon handle. Or if you're using an oval cooker, turn the lid sideways.

6. Cook on High for 1 hour, stirring up from the bottom and around the sides every 20 minutes or so. (Set a timer so you don't forget!)

7. Switch the cooker to Low. Bake another 1–2 hours, still stirring every 20 minutes or so.

8. Granola is done when it eventually browns a bit and looks dry.

9. Pour granola onto parchment or a large baking sheet to cool and crisp up more.

10. Stir in raisins.

11. If you like clumps, no need to stir further granola while it cools. Otherwise, break up the granola with a spoon or your hands as it cools.

12. When completely cooled, store in airtight container.

Sunflower Granola

Makes 8–10 servings

Prep. Time: 15–20 minutes ❦ Cooking Time: 2–3 hours ❦ Chilling Time: 1 hour

Ideal slow-cooker size: 6-quart

2 cups brown sugar, packed

6 cups dry oats, quick *or* rolled

2 cups wheat flour

1 cup wheat germ

2 cups unsweetened shredded coconut

1½ cups sunflower seeds

1 cup cooking oil

1 cup water

2 Tbsp. vanilla

1 tsp. salt

1. Grease interior of slow cooker crock.

2. In a large bowl, combine brown sugar, dry oats, wheat flour, wheat germ, coconut, and sunflower seeds.

3. When well mixed, stir in oil, water, vanilla, and salt. Stir well, remembering to stir up from the bottom, using either a strong spoon or your clean hands.

4. Pour mixture into crock. Cover, but vent the lid by propping it open with a chopstick or wooden spoon handle. Or if you're using an oval cooker, turn the lid sideways.

5. Cook on High for 1 hour, stirring up from the bottom and around the sides every 20 minutes or so. (Set a timer so you don't forget!)

6. Switch the cooker to Low. Bake another 1–2 hours, still stirring every 20 minutes or so.

7. Granola is done when it eventually browns a bit and looks dry.

8. Pour granola onto parchment or a large baking sheet to cool and crisp up more.

9. If you like clumps, no need to stir it while it cools. Otherwise, break up the granola with a spoon or your hands as it cools.

10. When completely cooled, store in airtight container.

TIP

Bake longer for crunchier cereal. Then let it cool completely for optimum crunch.

Peanut Butter Granola Surprise

Makes 9 servings

Prep. Time: 15 minutes ❧ Cooking Time: 2–3 hours ❧ Chilling Time: 30–60 minutes
Ideal slow-cooker size: 5- or 6-quart

8 Tbsp. (1 stick) butter, cut in chunks

½ cup apple juice concentrate, thawed

1 cup peanut butter, smooth *or* chunky

¾ cup brown sugar, packed

6 cups dry oats, quick *or* rolled

1. Put butter, apple juice concentrate, peanut butter, and brown sugar in a microwave-safe bowl.

2. Mic on High for 45 seconds. Stir. Continue cooking for 30-second intervals, stirring in between, until mixture melts together.

3. Put oats in large bowl and pour melted mixture over top. Stir well, including up from the bottom, until all oats are covered well. Or use your hands to mix.

4. Grease interior of slow cooker crock. Pour in oats mixture.

5. Cover, but vent the lid by propping it open with a chopstick or wooden spoon handle. Or if you're using an oval cooker, turn the lid sideways.

6. Cook on High for 1 hour, stirring up from the bottom and around the sides every 20 minutes or so. (Set a timer so you don't forget!)

7. Switch the cooker to Low and bake another 1–2 hours, still stirring every 20 minutes or so.

8. When granola has eventually browned a bit and looks dry, pour granola onto parchment or a large baking sheet to cool and crisp up more.

9. If you like clumps, no need to stir it while it cools. Otherwise, break it up with a spoon or your hands as it cools.

10. When completely cooled, store in airtight container.

Some great variations—

1. Stir in ½ cup raisins and ½ cup sunflower seeds as the granola cools in Step 9.

2. Serve it with milk or yogurt for breakfast. Or serve it over ice cream as a snack or dessert.

Lotsa Good Granola

Makes 9–10 servings

Prep. Time: 15–20 minutes ❧ Cooking Time: 2–3 hours ❧ Chilling Time: 1 hour

Ideal slow-cooker size: 6-quart

7 cups dry rolled oats

2½ cups whole wheat flour

½ cup sesame seeds

1 cup shredded unsweetened coconut

½ cup chopped almonds

1 cup wheat germ

¾ cup cooking oil

1 tsp. salt

½ cup brown sugar, packed

½ cup honey

½ cup water

1½ tsp. vanilla

1½ tsp. maple flavoring

1 cup chopped dates

1 cup raisins

1. Grease interior of slow cooker crock.

2. Combine oats, flour, sesame seeds, coconut, almonds, and wheat germ in a large bowl.

3. In a blender or food processor, combine oil, salt, brown sugar, honey, water, vanilla, and maple flavoring. Process until mixture turns to liquid.

4. Pour liquid over dry mixture. Add dates and raisins.

5. Stir well, remembering to stir up from the bottom, using either a strong spoon or your clean hands.

6. Pour mixture into crock. Cover, but vent the lid by propping it open with a chopstick or wooden spoon handle. Or if you're using an oval cooker, turn the lid sideways.

7. Cook on High for 1 hour, stirring up from the bottom and around the sides every 20 minutes or so. (Set a timer so you don't forget!)

8. Switch the cooker to Low. Bake another 1–2 hours, still stirring every 20 minutes or so.

9. Granola is done when it eventually browns a bit and looks dry.

10. Pour granola onto parchment or a large baking sheet to cool and crisp up more.

11. If you like clumps, no need to stir it while it cools. Otherwise, break up the granola with a spoon or your hands as it cools.

12. When completely cooled, store in airtight container.

Some great variations—

There's room for variations here. You can swap in another kind of nut. You can use chopped figs instead of dates. And Craisins® or dried plums for the raisins.

Apple Granola

Makes 6 servings

Prep. Time: 20 minutes ❧ Cooking Time: 1½–2 hours ❧ Chilling time: 1 hour

Ideal slow-cooker size: 5-quart

9 cups unpeeled, sliced apples

1½ tsp. cinnamon

1½ cups dry rolled oats

1½ cups wheat germ

1½ cups whole wheat flour

1½ cups sunflower seeds

1⅓ cups water

¾ cup honey

1. Grease interior of slow cooker crock.

2. Use your food processor to slice the apples. Place slices in crock.

3. Sprinkle apple slices with cinnamon, and then stir together gently.

4. In a good-sized bowl, stir together dry oats, wheat germ, whole wheat flour, and sunflower seeds.

5. When dry ingredients are well mixed, pour in water and honey. Using a sturdy spoon or your clean hands, mix thoroughly until wet ingredients are damp throughout.

6. Spoon over apples.

7. Cover, but vent the lid by propping it open with a chopstick or wooden spoon handle. Or if you're using an oval cooker, turn the lid sideways.

7. Cook on High for 1 hour, stirring up from the bottom and around the sides every 20 minutes or so. (Set a timer so you don't forget!)

8. Switch the cooker to Low. Bake another 1–2 hours, still stirring every 20 minutes or so.

9. Granola is done when it eventually browns a bit and looks dry.

10. Pour granola onto parchment or a large baking sheet to cool and crisp up more.

11. If you like clumps, no need to stir further granola while it cools. Otherwise, break up the granola with a spoon or your hands as it cools.

12. When completely cooled, store in airtight container.

Why I like this recipe—

If you can't wait to eat until the granola is cooled, help yourself to a bowl while it's still warm and top it with milk or yogurt.

Fall Fruits Granola

Makes 6–7 servings

Prep. Time: 20 minutes ❧ Cooking Time: 2–3 hours ❧ Chilling Time: 1–2 hours
Ideal slow-cooker size: 5- or 6-quart

½ cup honey

⅔ cup applesauce

3½ cups dry rolled oats

½ cup wheat germ

½ cup powdered milk

1 Tbsp. pumpkin pie spice

½ cup shredded unsweetened coconut

¼ cup soya flour

½ cup sunflower seeds

½ cup chopped nuts, your favorite

¼ cup sesame seeds

½ cup pumpkin seeds

¼ tsp. salt

Why I like this recipe—

I'm a texture nut, so I can't let this combination of seeds, nuts, and coconut alone. Plus it keeps me satisfied between breakfast and lunch. Funny what a tablespoon of pumpkin pie spice does to make you think holidays!

1. Grease interior of slow cooker crock.

2. In a microwave-safe bowl, or in a small saucepan, warm honey and applesauce together until you can easily blend them. Set aside.

3. In a good-sized bowl, mixt together oats, wheat germ powdered milk, pumpkin pie spice, coconut, flour, sunflower seeds, chopped nuts, sesame seeds, pumpkin seeds, and salt.

4. Pour wet ingredients over dry and combine well. Mix up from the bottom and stir in from the sides.

5. Pour mixture into slow cooker crock. Cover, but vent the lid by propping it open with a chopstick or wooden spoon handle. Or if you're using an oval cooker, turn the lid sideways.

6. Cook on High for 1 hour, stirring up from the bottom and around the sides every 20 minutes or so. (Set a timer so you don't forget!)

7. Switch the cooker to Low. Bake another 1–2 hours, still stirring every 20 minutes or so. Granola is done when it eventually browns a bit and looks dry.

8. Pour granola onto parchment or a large baking sheet to cool and crisp up more.

9. If you like clumps, no need to stir further it while it cools. Otherwise, continue to break up the granola with a spoon or your hands as it cools.

10. When completely cooled, store in airtight container.

Fruity Granola

Makes 7 hours

Prep. Time: 20 minutes ❧ Cooking Time: 2–3 hours
Ideal slow-cooker size: 4- or 5-quart

4 cups rolled dry oats

2 cups puffed rice cereal

½ cup shredded sweetened coconut

½ cup oat bran

¼ cup sliced almonds, toasted

¾ cup pineapple juice

½ cup apple juice

½ cup honey

⅓ cup dried blueberries

1. Grease interior of slow cooker crock.

2. In a good sized bowl, stir together dry oats, rice cereal, coconut, oat bran, and toasted sliced almonds.

3. Place pineapple and apple juices in a small saucepan. Heat to a boil, and then simmer until reduced to ⅔ cup. Watch carefully so it doesn't cook dry.

4. Stir honey into reduced juices.

5. Pour over dry ingredients, stirring until well combined.

6. Pour mixture into crock. Cover, but vent the lid by propping it open with a chopstick or wooden spoon handle. Or if you're using an oval cooker, turn the lid sideways.

7. Cook on High for 1 hour, stirring up from the bottom and around the sides every 20 minutes or so. (Set a timer so you don't forget!)

8. Switch the cooker to Low. Bake another 1–2 hours, still stirring every 20 minutes or so. Granola is done when it eventually browns a bit and looks dry.

9. Pour granola onto parchment or a large baking sheet to cool and crisp up more.

10. Stir in dried blueberries when it's almost cool to room temperature. If you like clumps, no need to stir further it while it cools. Otherwise, continue to break up the granola with a spoon or your hands as it cools.

11. When completely cooled, store in airtight container.

Why I like this recipe—

You see what's happening here, right? You've used fruit juices instead of oil in this light and fruity combination!

Keep It Lowfat Granola

Makes 5–6 servings

Prep. Time: 15–20 minutes ❧ *Cooking Time: 2–3 hours* ❧ *Chilling Time: 1 hour*

Ideal slow-cooker size: 5-quart

2 eggs

1 Tbsp. + 1 tsp. baking powder

2 cups skim milk

2 cups brown sugar, packed

4 cups dry oats, quick *or* rolled

1 cup dry bran, wheat *or* oat

1½ cups cornmeal

1 tsp. salt

1. Grease interior of slow cooker crock.

2. Mix all ingredients together in crock, stirring up from the bottom with either a sturdy spoon or your clean hands.

3. Cover, but vent the lid by propping it open with a chopstick or wooden spoon handle. Or if you're using an oval cooker, turn the lid sideways.

4. Cook on High for 1 hour, stirring up from the bottom and around the sides every 20 minutes or so. (Set a timer so you don't forget!)

5. Switch the cooker to Low. Bake another 1–2 hours, still stirring every 20 minutes or so.

6. Granola is done when it eventually browns a bit and looks dry.

7. Pour granola onto parchment or a large baking sheet to cool and crisp up more.

8. If you like clumps, no need to stir it while it cools. Otherwise, break up the granola with a spoon or your hands as it cools.

9. When completely cooled, store in airtight container.

Why I like this recipe—

The eggs add a different consistency to this granola—plus also protein. And the cornmeal brings its own flavor. Top your bowl with chopped fresh fruit or berries.

Soy-Flax Granola

Makes 10 servings
Prep. Time: 20 minutes ❦ Cooking Time: 1½–2½ hours ❦ Chilling Time: 2 hours
Ideal slow-cooker size: 6-quart

12 oz. soybeans, roasted with no salt

4 cups dry rolled oats

¾ cup soy flour

¾ cup ground flax seed

1¼ cups brown sugar

1 tsp. salt

2 tsp. cinnamon

⅔ cup coarsely chopped walnuts

⅔ cup whole pecans

½ cup vegetable oil

¾ cup applesauce

2 tsp. vanilla

dried cranberries, dried cherries, chopped dried apricots, chopped dried figs, raisins, *or* some combination of these dried fruits *optional*

1. Grease interior of slow cooker crock.

2. Briefly process soybeans in a blender or food processor until coarsely chopped. Place in large bowl.

3. Add oats, flour, flax seed, brown sugar, salt, cinnamon, walnuts, and pecans. Mix thoroughly with spoon, breaking up any brown sugar lumps.

4. In a smaller bowl, combine oil, applesauce, and vanilla well.

5. Pour wet ingredients over dry. Stir well, remembering to stir up from the bottom, using either a strong spoon or your clean hands.

6. Pour mixture into crock. Cover, but vent the lid by propping it open with a chopstick or wooden spoon handle. Or if you're using an oval cooker, turn the lid sideways.

7. Cook on High for 1 hour, stirring up from the bottom and around the sides every 20 minutes or so. (Set a timer so you don't forget!)

8. Switch the cooker to Low. Bake another 1–2 hours, still stirring every 20 minutes or so.

9. Granola is done when it eventually browns a bit and looks dry.

10. Pour granola onto parchment or a large baking sheet to cool and crisp up more.

11. Stir in any of the dried fruits that you want.

12. If you like clumps, no need to stir further granola while it cools. Otherwise, break up the granola with a spoon or your hands as it cools.

13. When completely cooled, store in airtight container.

TIP

1. You can be flexible with this granola's dry ingredients. Just keep the dry/wet proportions similar. 2. We love to eat this topped with yogurt and fresh fruit. It's kind of like dessert for breakfast.

Metric Equivalent Measurements

If you're accustomed to using metric measurements, I don't want you to be inconvenienced by the imperial measurements I use in this book.

Use this handy chart, too, to figure out the size of the slow cooker you'll need for each recipe.

Weight *(Dry Ingredients)*

1 oz		30 g
4 oz	¼ lb	120 g
8 oz	½ lb	240 g
12 oz	¾ lb	360 g
16 oz	1 lb	480 g
32 oz	2 lbs	960 g

Slow Cooker Sizes

1-quart	0.96 l
2-quart	1.92 l
3-quart	2.88 l
4-quart	3.84 l
5-quart	4.80 l
6-quart	5.76 l
7-quart	6.72 l
8-quart	7.68 l

Volume *(Liquid Ingredients)*

½ tsp.		2 ml
1 tsp.		5 ml
1 Tbsp.	½ fl oz	15 ml
2 Tbsp.	1 fl oz	30 ml
¼ cup	2 fl oz	60 ml
⅓ cup	3 fl oz	80 ml
½ cup	4 fl oz	120 ml
⅔ cup	5 fl oz	160 ml
¾ cup	6 fl oz	180 ml
1 cup	8 fl oz	240 ml
1 pt	16 fl oz	480 ml
1 qt	32 fl oz	960 ml

Length

¼ in	6 mm
½ in	13 mm
¾ in	19 mm
1 in	25 mm
6 in	15 cm
12 in	30 cm

Substitute Ingredients for When You're in a Pinch—

For one cup **buttermilk**—use 1 cup plain yogurt, or pour 1⅓ Tbsp. lemon juice or vinegar into a 1-cup measure. Fill the cup with milk. Stir and let stand for 5 minutes. Stir again before using.

For 1 oz. **unsweetened baking chocolate**—stir together 3 Tbsp. unsweetened cocoa powder and 1 Tbsp. butter, softened.

For 1 Tbsp. **cornstarch**—use 2 Tbsp. all-purpose flour, or 4 tsp. minute tapioca.

For 1 cup **sour milk**—use 1 cup plain yogurt, or pour 1 Tbsp. lemon juice or vinegar into a 1-cup measure. Fill with milk. Stir and then let stand for 5 minutes. Stir again before using.

For 1 cup **heavy cream**—add ⅓ cup melted butter to ¾ cup milk. **Note:** *This will work for baking and cooking, but not for whipping.*

For 1 cup **whipping cream**—chill thoroughly ⅔ cup evaporated milk, plus the bowl and beaters, then whip, or use 2 cups bought whipped topping.

Recipe and Ingredient Index

Recipe and Ingredient Index ❦ **325**

About the Author —

Phyllis Good is a *New York Times* bestselling author whose books have sold more than 12 million copies.

She authored *Fix-It and Forget-It Cookbook, Revised and Updated*, which appeared on *The New York Times* bestseller list, as well as the bestseller lists of *USA Today*, *Publishers Weekly*, and Book Sense. In addition, she authored *Fix-It and Forget-It Lightly* (which also appeared on *The New York Times* bestseller list); as well as *Fix-It and Forget-It Christmas Cookbook*; *Fix-It and Forget-It 5-Ingredient Favorites*; *Fix-It and Forget-It Vegetarian Cookbook*; *Fix-It and Forget-It Diabetic Cookbook, Revised and Updated* (with the American Diabetes Association); *Fix-It and Forget-It Big Cookbook*; *Fix-It and Forget-It Kids Cookbook*; *Fix-It and Forget-It New Cookbook*; and *Fix-It and Forget-It Slow Cooker Magic*.

Good's commitment is to make it possible for everyone to cook who would like to, even if they have too little time or too little confidence.

Good has authored many other cookbooks. Among them are *Fix-It and Enjoy-It Healthy Cookbook* (with nutritional expertise from Mayo Clinic), *The Best of Amish Cooking*, and *Lancaster Central Market Cookbook*.

Good spends her time writing on a variety of subjects, editing books, and cooking new recipes.